MW01595237

ISBN 9781096801832

June 2019

Cover design: Cynthia M. Ruiz

"The purpose of the book is to share the lessons I have learned in my life in hopes that it can make a positive difference in the world and inspire others to their greatness."

Oscar "Big O" Dillon

Forward

Oscar "Big O" Dillon has lived many lives as a Sports Figure, Professional Martial Artist, Personal Trainer, Body Builder, Musician, Singer, Police officer, Street Detective, Celebrity Body Guard, Stunt Man, Actor and Motivational Speaker.

God has given him another chance to share his heart and knowledge with the world. While he was St. Louis Police Officer/Detective he saved many lives and put the bad guys where they belonged.

His police work and real life experiences laid the foundation for him to become an actor in Hollywood, where play various roles and characters on the big screen.

Today he uses his life's journey to help others though his motivational speaking.

Dedication

I'm inspired to write this book for people to never give up. If you give in and be humble to God, and put him first, only then you will see he has had a plan for you all along. You just couldn't see it.

Lord, thank you for a little extra time on this earth. I died not just once but twice, that is why I know my work on this planet is not yet finished.

God needs my voice to reach more people with his message. I have realized we have to give back to society.

This life is not ours to keep the ultimate in this life is to be of service to God and all humanity. First and foremost this book is dedicated to God the creator of all.

Next I dedicate this book to my parents Hazel Marie and Oscar Dillon Sr. your love; teachings and struggles have lifted me.

Shout out to all my family and friends for your love and support over the years. Too many people to name and I don't want to leave anybody out, but you know whom you are. You have inspired me to be the man I am today and will continue to be.

My beautiful soul sister Cynthia M. Ruiz, who God always puts into my life at the perfect time, thanks for your hard work in getting this project over the finish line and designing the amazing book cover.

I also am grateful for all of the angels God had put in my life along my journey there are too many to name but special recognition goes to the nurse who did not leave my side after I died and came back. She would not leave my side until she was sure I was going to survive.

A special thanks to Dr. Mary Reid Gaudio, for her listening ear and inspiration while we were working together.

Special shout out to all my colleagues in the entertainment field, it really does take a community to make the magic happen.

Also a special thanks to my dear friends and business associates at Ontrix Solutions.

To all the people in my life be blessed and know I appreciate your support along the way.

OSCAR DILLO
SAG / AFTRA
(BIG O)

A Message from Oscar

I feel so blessed to have had so many great experiences in my life. As I have been able to accomplish so much and meet so many amazing people along the way.

I even appreciate the challenges, good and bad since they were instrumental in shaping me into the man I am today.

My mission is to help others but I particularly want to help the men be men and the boys become men with integrity.

I look around and see so many men not knowing how to deal with their feelings or emotions and they take their anger out on other people in various ways. Shootings, bombings and overall violence have become far too common, **THAT CLEARLY IS NOT THE ANSWER!**

Let us come together and make this world a better place. I understand that it all starts with each of us as individuals, so with that, I humbly share my life lessons with you.

I have learned many lessons in my life and would like to share the five most important:

1) To really be strong means to willingly and humbly **Surrender to God**. The only way to get there is to put your ego aside and be humble. Always put God first! Yes, when you put God first all the time you will reap the rewards. Many people call on God when they are in need, disappointed, angry or desperate. Once you put him first he will light the way. This is not to say you will not have challenges, we all do. Challenges are put in our life so we can learn lessons from them. Throughout my life people would look at my muscles and think that is what made me strong, which is only surface stuff. My real strength came to me when I was strong enough to surrender.

2) You can have it all if you are willing to **work** for it. I have been able to accomplish things I only dreamed about as a

child. There was no quick path to success and no one handed me anything on a silver platter. My journey has been filled with Blood, Sweat and a lot of tears. I put in the hours, days, weeks and years of hard work. You too can reach your dreams if you are willing to put in the effort.

3) Be **persistent and never give up**. What I have been able to accomplish has been through hard work and discipline. On the days I wanted to give up I kept going. In my darkest moments I knew the sun would once again shine. I have been on the doorstep of death (not once but twice) only to return with purpose and passion.

4) **Life is about making good choices**. Because of my life long passion for fitness I made choices about what I was putting into my body and made a choice to be discipline. I choose to have consistent fitness routine in place. When one door closed, I made a choice to go in a different direction but kept moving forward.

5) The real meaning of being a man, first being true to oneself and desiring to **helping others**. Surrendering to God has given me a clear understanding that we are all connected and we are all part of the human race. As a man I know that my job is to help others and make this world a better place. It is not about having the fancy cars, the biggest houses or hottest women by your side. It is about being of service to your family, community and the world around you.

Contents

"Don't chase people. Be yourself, do your own thing and work hard. The right people- the ones who really belong in your life- will come to you. And stay."

Will Smith

Chapter 1
Code Blue

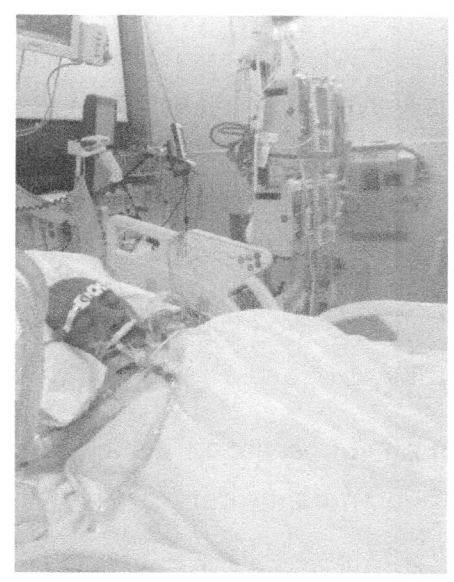

When I woke from a code blue I felt like I had been in a state of euphoria. I had no idea how long I was out but the first thing I remember when I opened my eyes is people repeatedly calling my name, Oscar, Oscar wake up. Wow, I think I just watched my life pass in front of my eyes, Oh My God I heard people screaming saying we lost him. That it when I realized I had died and came back.

Once I was released from the hospital people starting asking me, where I've been hiding? Where've you been? The word on the street is you had died. We haven't seen you for at least ten years. Some people didn't even think you were on this earth anymore. You know how some people just disappear off the face of the earth and then magically reappear? That's you! So what happened?

You really want to hear? I'm going to tell you the whole story, from my very beginning till right now.

 Are you ready? Put on your seatbelt, it's a wild ride, sometimes bumpy even. But I guarantee it's not going to be boring.

My unforeseen medical challenges began surfaced in the beginning of 2008. I had just finished shooting a movie with Carol Burnette. It was her comeback movie. Michael Keaton and Alexis Bledel were also in it. The film title was Post Grad. I was working sixteen-hour days and was a little tired because of long hours. I was still training hard and I was in good shape. I felt a little fatigue, heaviness, and I didn't make too much about it. Two other films were being discussed at the same time. They were in the making and they were interested in me. They wanted me to get a physical. That prompted me to make an appointment with my doctor. Just as I was getting ready to walk to the exit the doctor approached me. I had been waiting for the blood test to come back. I'd been sitting there for a while and I was ready to leave. They also did x-rays and the doctor wanted to tell me about them.

The doctor said, "Mr. Dillon, hold on a second. Can you have a seat for a minute?"

"Yeah, why, is something up?"

"I'm not sure but just have a seat for a minute. I'll get back to you in a minute."

He came back with about six other doctors. They had their long white coats on and they're standing in front of me, looking at me with their eyebrows scrunched like they were amazed at something. They were looking and whispering to each other.

I said, "What's up?"

"We found something interesting. We were reviewing your x-rays again and we found an unexplained cloud of fluid in your chest."

They showed me where it was on the x-ray screen.

"I see something in your blood that's not normal. And the unexplained fluid in your chest is not normal. We don't know how you're still standing here. What we see is that you've had not one but two significant heart attacks. How do you feel?"

My legs got weak. A metamorphosis just took place.

"A little tired but I've been working some long days."

Now I'm frozen in my tracks. I was stunned. I was in disbelief.

"Your ejection fraction is way under what it should be for life."

That's how your heart fires, like the motor of a car. The spark plugs are hitting on the right cylinder. Your heart is beating way too slow for normal. It's like starting a dead battery on a car.

"I brought in these other doctors because I'm baffled on how you're standing here alive. You should be dead, buried, but you're standing here talking to us. We've never seen something like this before."

They couldn't pinpoint when I had the heart attacks but they knew that I had two. I don't remember having one, or two for that matter. Now I'm trying to figure out when that could have happened?

"The only reason why you're not dead is that you have this amazing Herculean, Samson kind of body that has held you up. It's like a house with a great foundation. It's been carrying that weak heart for some time. I don't know how long but it didn't happen today."

I'm thinking, who's the guy who was playing jokes on people all the time, Ashton Kutcher? Am I being punked? When's the guy going to come around with the camera? I did a couple of those where I played the investigator. Suddenly I'm hearing sirens.

The doctor said, "Hear those sirens? They're coming for you. We already called them."

I was at the Motion Picture Hospital in Calabasas on Mulholland. The ambulance came with ten firemen with gurneys. It was like we were on the set of a big fire.

They ran past me to the doctors, "Where's our patient?"

"He's behind you."

"We got a call that you had a heart attack trauma patient. That's him?

But he's standing...But he looks like... You're the patient?"

"They say I am."

"Well, we need to put you on this gurney then."

"I can walk out."

"No, we want you to lay on the gurney. We need to strap you down and we were told to get you to the fastest and nearest trauma center."

The Fire Department ambulance took me to West Hills Hospital. It was six minutes away by running every red light and driving like a police pursuit. It seemed like a bad movie.

I said, "Do you have to drive so fast?"

It was like that movie *Speed* with Sandra Bullock and Keanu Reeves. I was holding on for dear life.

"Dude, when we get you there will be a whole trauma team waiting for you outside."

We rolled up and all these doctors and nurses jumped into action. They hooked me up to life support machines. They were trying to save my life because they were told that I could die at any second.

They said, "The next heart attack would traumatic and we probably couldn't save you."

They didn't say any minute, they said any second.

I said, "This is not happening to me. This can't be happening to me."

They put me on another gurney and began cutting my clothes off and hooking machines up to me.

"We appreciate if you don't talk because we have to put this oxygen mask on you and you are being connected to a defibrillator."

I'm basically in shock. I don't know what to say anymore and I'm just rolling with it. They checked me into a room and then I was able to have someone call my mother. My girlfriend at the time, Cindy, was waiting in the lobby and was later directed to my room.

I said, "Is this really happening?"

Cindy said, "I knew something was wrong with you. You were breathing heavy and you'd drop your head sometimes watching TV and you would stop breathing."

I knew I had sleep apnea but didn't think it was a big deal. Occasionally I would stop breathing which woke me up. Now I think this might have been related to the heart attacks.

I went to the hospital on Valentine's Day. How about that? This occurred in February 2008. That was my valentine, and it had to do with my heart, ironically. For over a month I was lying in the hospital while the doctors were baffled about how best to approach my situation.

They did twenty to thirty different tests to see where the fluid came from. You can't do surgery on someone if you don't know exactly how to approach it. They put me on all these diuretics to get the fluid out of me. They said if they cut me open with all the fluid in me that I would die instantly. Afterward, we'll do some tests and see what the source was. If we operate now, you're not going to make it.

They put me in an Indian Scan Machine, which was like an MRI. It was like a space capsule as it was spinning around me. It was making a bunch of noise. I was in there for an hour and they still weren't sure that they found the source.

The machine found some blockage in my mouth. He said you do have a badly impacted wisdom tooth, which was infected. The wisdom tooth is in a place where normal dental machines can't see it. It was up by my upper jaw and ear. It was basically hiding in the gum.

I didn't have a toothache but I had a little bit of misconfiguration here. Some of us have a little bit of difference from one side of our face to the other. I have a round face but someone asked a couple times if my jaw was swollen.

I said, "No, not really."

My tooth could have been leaking into my heart for years, it could have been any of number of things. From my physical work or stress as a cop. I had a crazy cop life but I never spoke about it. Only a few guys knew about it. We had a team called TACT-Tactical Anti-Crime Team, which was a special force assigned by the Chief of Police and the St. Louis Police Department. I was a part of the team and we went under cover. We got people for murder, rape, robbery, serial killers, child molesters, drug dealers- not the little guys but the big guys. My life was in danger every day. This was really my acting training at the time. That's why I just walked into this business. I used all my voices. When I was a child, I mimicked people. It got me my nickname, Jerry Lewis. I even used to do his funny antics. It just didn't dawn on me. Life was my acting school. I was on the streets reading people and that's what a good actor does. The best acting class was living in the ghetto. There were no pagers, no cell phones. Once you leave your house you're on your own.

I'm back now. I'm well. I was gone and I couldn't tell anybody. I couldn't function. I didn't know what the next day was going to bring. I didn't know if there was going to be a next day and there almost wasn't. Dr. Gharabi was my doctor. Somewhere in there I heard them say, 'Code Blue. We lost him. ' I heard them. Then I heard the heart alarm go off on the machine.

I was clinically dead I guess.

Suddenly, I'm looking down at myself back on the operating table again. I can't believe this ride I'm on. The doctors and nurses are all around me but I can't call out. No one can hear me. When I've heard other people tell these stories, everyone is different slightly, similar yet different. I didn't know. How do you know what death is until you actually experience it. You can't compare it to someone else's near death or death experience. Yours is your own individual situation. The light is similar. A lot of people talk about the light. But entering that light and what you saw and heard, where you were and how you feel you got there, the last thing you remember, is a different story by each person. In my situation, I told the anesthesiologist to give me the shot. Then I was gone. Somewhere in that period of time I heard, 'We lost him' then 'Code blue' and then I heard the beeping. That was the first time I died.

I don't know how long it was. I don't know how long I was under. It must be when I was reminiscing about my childhood. Apparently, it wasn't too long because if you go under too long your brain is dead. In fact, I signed a piece of paper saying in many cases for quad bypass surgery, the person comes back with brain damage from the surgery. This bypass surgery was in 2008. As you can see, it didn't go quite right. I passed away and they brought me back. They opened me up a second time. I passed away a second time. Someone called out Code Blue again. This must be the second Code Blue I'm on now. They worked on the quad some more and got me stable, or so they thought.

It's in the bible. (Philippians 4:7) And the peace of God, which transcends all understanding, will guard your hearts and your minds in Christ Jesus. When I came back from my second flat line, those words, that scripture entered my mind because it was such an experience that you can't find the words for it. I don't think there are any words to fit the feeling of euphoria/ floating in the air, peaceful. All I could hear was a soft wind sound like you're way out in the country on a mountain somewhere-or falling out of a space ship. You're close to God, nature. You don't hear anything. There's a slight wind and all the stars are lit up. There's no one around in the whole world but you. You just hear a whisper in the wind. I felt very safe and if I could put it in a photo it's like when we were first born, swaddled in a blanket like Jesus was, feeling content and quiet. It was that kind of feeling but it was you as a man.

Men have a hard time surrendering. We're not taught how to surrender. I was taught by my mom and dad to trust God, which leads you to the ability to surrender. I think that's what makes us surrender to love. We feel that if you trust the person, all the stuff that you went through before in your life slowly leaves you. This person you love brings a calm and peace you never had before. You just have to say Thank You Jesus.

The first time I died, it seemed to take a short time to get me back and I felt sudden peace. They had to reopen my chest. This is the second time I saw the white light. I went from tense to calm and this time there were three words that God said to me in a reverberating booming voice, like an electric guitar ringing, singing in the clouds, so magical and mesmerizing, so soothing-

'I AM HERE.'

That shook me to my core but I felt safe- in his arms, completely OK. I could have just stayed there for eternity. This didn't last though, fortunately. I was jolted back to earth and reality. But God was with me on earth. I felt his presence constantly and I had a direct connection with him daily. I prayed, I worshipped, I sang. I was confident that God wasn't going to desert me. I was given another chance to live and share what I've learned.

But now back to the hospital. I had a different doctor a day or two later. I had to walk around the hospital and do the stairs. This was unusual. I wanted to get out of there immediately.

"The food isn't working here at all. It's going to kill me."

The nurse said, "This is our protocol meal. Everyone gets the same thing."

I said, "Look at me. Do I look like your protocol? Here's a picture of Conan."

"Oh my God, is that you?"

"That's me. That's who I am."

"I knew you looked familiar. We used to go to that show all the time."

I grumbled, 'Doc, how long will I be in here?"

"Well, what you just went through, you're looking at a good 7-8 days before you can go home."

He saw my face and changed his tune, "If you can walk around the perimeter of the hospital floor and do one flight of stairs, then you can go home."

"Oh, yeah, let's go."

With a watchful eye, all the doctors and nurses on that floor were observing me as I did my walk in disbelief, and I did it twice.

I came back and said, "Let's do the stairs."

I went back to my room and all was quiet.

The doctors were shocked, "He did not just do that!"

I was able to go home in six days rather than eight days after surgery. I saw a different cardiologist in Tarzana, Woodland Hills, and then Whittier. The Whittier doctor sent me to Cedar Sinai. Dr. Howard Elkin, from Whittier, was a body builder.

Dr. Elkin reluctantly stated, "I've done all that I can do. You're beyond me and you need to see a team of the greatest cardiologists in the world. Some of them are my friends. You need to go see them. Specifically, I'd like you to see my friend that I golf with, Dr. Jaime Moraguchi."

In 2009-2010, I went to Cedars. I offered to train the doctors who were out of shape. I gave them advice as they were working on me. They told me I had a pretty amazing knowledge about the body. Why aren't you a doctor? I did want to be as a young boy, but I was into bodybuilding and pro football. I still study the body, literally every day. I study the concept of putting the body together from the inside out, not the outside in. Once you learn what's going on inside of you. That's where it begins.

I feel like I'm floating and it's heavenly. I'm not ready to wake up yet. I can't believe it's me we're talking about.

What a crazy ride I'm living!

"Everyone can rise above their circumstances and achieve success if they are dedicated to and passionate about what they do"

Nelson Mandela

Chapter 2

YOUNG BIG O

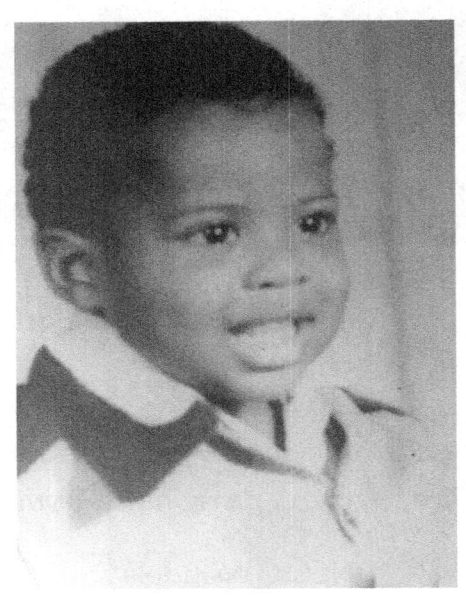

HOW'D YOU GET THAT WAY?

Going up in St Louis I came from a devoted Christian family. We went to church every Sunday. There were six of us; I originally had three sisters and two brothers.

I grew up surrounded by music my Dad was a talented singer and guitar player; my Mom was also a talented musician, singing and playing piano.

My first memory is being a toddler walking around the house using the broom as a pretend guitar. My parents looked at me and said, yes this boy is meant to play an instrument and they bought me my first guitar when I was three or four years old. My Dad encouraged to me to practice everyday. Even at a young age he saw greatness in me.

I was in the choir… singing and all that. I played bass. I was a skinny young kid. I played for everybody. I just ate it up. My dad played bass, too. He had a band called The Trumpets. He played with his brothers. I would play with my dad's band when I was a young boy. My dad played and sang. My dad was superman in so many ways. He could build this house. He could tear a car apart. He created his own business and then he went back to school as an older man. He got his degree and opened his business up. He worked two jobs and raised six kids.

He and my mom were so in love. They did everything together. They used to wrestle and play in the house and throw pillows at each other. He would walk around the car and still open the door for her to get in. She would dress nicely for him at times.

I'd ask "Mom, where you going?"

She said, "Your dad will be home in a few minutes. You'll figure it out."

Every man wants the whole package. We saw that and we became that. That was our environment every day. And no one eats before we pray. Then we had bible study every Wednesday night-without fail. There was no doing what we want, she fixed a meal... and I said, "But mom I want..."

She said, "No, no, no, I fixed food... I made these potatoes, and guess what? My kids are not going to do that. I'm going to feed them healthy food so they can grow up and be strong and healthy."

When I was six or seven years old, up in the trees, my mom asked me, "Boy, what are you doing up there?"

"I'm doing pull ups so I can be strong."

I had to find a limb so it was horizontal so I could do pull-ups and it was way up top. My bedroom was on the third floor in the old house and I climbed up there to the third floor and went down to the second and jumped on the tree branch. I did pull ups, then back in the house, then do pushups in the basement with two old rusty irons clothes irons. I used those for dumb bells because I didn't have any weights. I was too young and my mom wouldn't buy me any weights. She said your bones are too soft and you're going to hurt yourself. But I still did it anyway. I think every boy goes through a period. You get out of the shower. You look in the mirror. You make a muscle.

We were country people. We grew up on my grandmother's farm. She had a big farm with a big family. She had ten kids, and my mom had nine sisters. My dad had nine siblings himself. In all, I've got a lot of cousins. I'm used to big families.

There was a man that told me, after church service.., a man who was a minister named Holland... he was buff. He never took his coat off but you could see his muscles through his suit. He was a friend of my dad's and he told my aunt and my grandma to watch me.

He took my arm and he squeezed it and said, "We have to put some meat on them bones boy."

I said, "Let me see yours. I can tell you've got muscles even though you never took your jacket off."

I paused.

I said, "Would you take your jacket off for me?"

He said, "For you I will." He took his jacket off and rolled up his shirt. I was just BOOM! I want to be like that. I looked at his arm, at his body and I said, "That's me."

My dad said, "You like that huh?"

I said, "I like that Dad. That's what I want to be."

I already started when I was swinging and climbing and jumping in the tree. I want to be big and I want to be strong. I did, I became that. In my mom's house, I locked myself in the basement twice a day, before school and after school, every single day seven days a week. I'd be down there in the basement with clothes irons and pipes and two by fours, doing pull ups and sweating and looking in the mirror and going yeah, yeah.

My mom was sitting on the steps and I didn't know it. She was watching me. She could see what I was doing.

When I came back up my mom said, "Are you finished?"

I said, "Yeah."

"What are you trying to do?"

"I'm working out. Why, were you looking at me?"

"Yes"

"How long? How long were you sitting up there looking at me?"

"Long enough. Lord, what am I raising?" I said, "Guess what? Momma, when I get big I'm going to buy you a house. Nobody's going to mess with you. And them bills on the table, you won't have to cry about them no more."

That motivated me.

I went to Enright Middle School and became the National Spelling Bee Champion in the 7th and 8th grade. I got a trophy and my picture in the paper. I got good grades.

Then I went to Soldan, High School, home of the Tigers. I finished that and graduated. I played football and studied martial arts. I took class after school. I continued my music. I did body building shows and played bass with different choirs at different venues.

My dad would come home and say, "Honey, I don't have enough money to pay the bills. We'll just make some food. I know they're going to turn the lights off tomorrow. I'll pay it next payday. We'll be ok for a week."

Then when I came home, the lights weren't on and I'd say, "Mom where's the food?"

"I'll make you guys a peanut butter sandwich. That's all we got right now. Dad's going to bring something home later."

I'd say, "Mom, I'm tired of this." I kind of have a way with kids in that I used to be that poor kid.

I wanted to get out of the ghetto but couldn't because I didn't have money. I was subjected to the violence and the gangs.

This turned me, out of anger, into what I am today. I took my anger when my mom said; just try to dodge them when you can.

"Momma, I dodged, I ducked, I ran and they told me tomorrow I'm going to kill you if you don't give me any money on the way to school." I walked to school.

She said, "What are you doing?"

"I'm sticking nun-chucks down my sleeves."

I bought me some steel-toed boots for kicking purposes. I became a warrior. Like Stallone getting ready for Rambo. I was already a black belt. I was quiet, shy but I was angry inside.

My dad said, "Son, I know you, don't start anyhing. Finish it, finish it good. If you don't, they going to come back."

"I understand."

One day I came home all bloody. I hurt three or four guys up at the schoolyard 'cause they jumped me. I was like fourteen, thirteen.

At first I came home crying 'cause I was angry when that happened.

My mom was upset, "What's wrong with you?"

"You don't understand. I'm sick and tired of this." I had a gun but I didn't go there. I was a good kid" Momma, you can't help me.

You're baking and doing what you do. This is a neighborhood full of gang members and thugs and I'm tired of it."

"Son, we can't move. Dad doesn't make enough money and he's doing the best he can. In fact, we don't have any lights today and he doesn't get paid till next week. We don't have lights and we have one loaf of bread in the refrigerator and a couple slices of bologna. That's what you guys got for dinner."

"What? We don't have any food? No lights?"

I got angry.

"I'm telling you son. We need help. You need to get a job."

I went and lied about my age and got two jobs. I got a job shining shoes at a place called House of Good Care with Mr. Jerry. I was a little kid but I could pop that shoe shine rag. I had all these businessmen lined up to shine their shoes. I was good. I was passionate. I had all this anger coming out of me.

Then I got a job at Al Baker's Restaurant as a bus boy. I was fourteen. I lied and said I was sixteen. You can wait on tables but we're going to start you out as a bus boy first. I did that and they moved me up to being a waiter. That didn't turn out very well. I brought one big old tray like this to a table for a bunch of millionaires for a private dinner and the lady had a mink coat. Someone came around and brushed my elbow. I dumped everything from the tray on the table and it splashed all over her mink coat and her clothes.

They got up yelling, "Who's your boss?"

"I'll go get him."

The boss came to me and said, "You're done. You're fired. The paycheck you were getting… we're using that to pay for this. Get your stuff and go. You get nothing."

I didn't argue. I know that was a lot of money. I left there and I was angry. I kept saying this sucks. This just sucks. My dad needs money.

My dad said, "This is what you can do. I taught you how to fix cars so while I'm at my normal job, we can fix cars in the back of the garage. I've got some customers for you. I'm going to have you fix their cars while I'm at work. I'll finish. I showed you how to pull the transmission out and put it back in. Can you do that son?"

"Yes sir."

"If you have any problems, there's a manual right here called the mechanics manual. Everything you want to know is in there, or ask me a question." "I got it. I watched you daddy."

I was out there, and it's ten below zero outside.

"I need your help, son. If we get this done we'll have enough money to get the lights back on."

"Ok, daddy, I'm coming with you."

I put my earmuffs on 'cause snow was outside this deep. I'd go to the garage.

"What do you want me to do first?"

"Pull the heads off this thing. I'll get in and loosen the engine bolts. We'll have this out in no time."

I'd start. I was maybe sixteen. I learned all these things about cars and I became this great mechanic at a young age.

"Now, you're going to fix cars and when I come back from work I'll join you and we'll make money."

That's what we did for a little while.

My mom said, "Son, I'm trying. Your dad's working, he's the only one working and we're doing the best we can. Don't worry about this right now. Get your education, you're smart."

My dad sat me down and said, "Son, (he looked me in the eye) I want you to become great. Whatever you decide to do, be the best! And more than anything, learn diction. Learn to speak well."

It's not like I didn't, but he wanted me to be an educated Black man, someone like Sidney Poitier. Dad held him up as an example.

In my classes, I was on top in my English classes.

He said that's good to continue that but as a Black man, you're Black, it's against you. The world doesn't want to hire a man who seems to come from the street.

Dad said, "I'm here to check out the job. You know what I'm saying; you know what I'm saying? Don't be like that. Be proud, be educated because you know what?

Your mother's a third white, a third Cherokee Indian and a third Black."

She has pretty with black hair, and a great body.

My mom's hot! I said I want someone like you. She'd wear pretty knit dresses, and she would say, "This is for your dad." "I know."

She cooks and you know I love food.

She said, "When you get married someday, don't ever marry a woman who doesn't cook or who doesn't make you the most important person in the world. You're an special child and you'll be an amazing man so you need an amazing woman."

Oscar "Big O" High School

At 17, the first girl I was ever seeing said you're not going to get away and said, "You're mine. We're going to grow old together".

She was cute. She lived in the neighborhood. I was on the neighborhood baseball team and I was the MVP all the time and she'd come and sit in the bleachers and watch me hit home runs all the time.

She told all the girls "That's my man."

She was just a girl. She'd always go, "Hi Oscar" and I'd put my head down 'cause I was shy but I was a bad dude in sports and working out. Bottom line is I wound up seeing her and she enticed me into a physical relationship.

I was cute. I was muscular. All the girls wanted me but she thought she was going to put her stamp on me before they did. That's how young girls are when they want a cute kid. She was quiet and normal but she was aggressive because she didn't want anyone else to have me. A lot of girls were after me because of sports and all. I didn't know it but after we had that little run in some weeks later, she gave me some shocking news.

She said, "Guess what?"

I said "What?" "I missed my period."

I said, "OK."

"I think I'm pregnant."

I said, "What? How can you be pregnant? You're on birth control! You told me you took the birth control pill. I didn't watch you but you took the pill, didn't you?"

She said, "No, I lied to you. I wanted a baby. Whether you want it or not, I want your baby."

I said, "Aww man, why did you do that?"

"You don't have to stay if you don't want but I'm having this baby."

She told my mom and dad who were Christians that I'm having his baby and I want to marry him. My mom and dad thought it was sweet and she was beautiful.

I was sixteen going on seventeen.

She told my mom and dad, and I heard her, "I'm going to be a good wife to him. I'm going to cook and clean. He won't need any of these other girls."

That impressed my mother.

My girlfriend begged, "Will you tell him to marry me?"

My mom said, "Well, I'll talk to him."

My parents both had a meeting with me. Sitting at the table, I was wondering what was going on. My dad stated, "Son, there's obviously a situation going on here. You know your girlfriend's pregnant."

"That's what she says."

"You're going to have to marry her."

"But dad, I'm only seventeen."

My dad proudly explained, "I married your mom when I was sixteen and we had six of you guys."

He said, "That baby's going to need a father. Going to church with a baby and you're not married...in front of all those people... it would ruin the family name in the image of God. You'll marry her because that's who we are."

I said, "Really?"

Mom said, "That's right son. Your dad and I talked about it and we agree. You need to marry this girl."

We went to the courthouse. The baby came just before this. We didn't have a wedding; we just have a civil ceremony. I was standing there like I was being executed, with this look on my face. At the time, I had this big Afro.

And the judge said, "Mr. Dillon, do you take this woman…" and I was like…

I looked at her and she said, "Just say yah."

I was like, "Ummm, ummm… yes, okay."

It was done and we left. I was a married teenager. We had our itty bitty boy.

We remained married, off and on. We were married by paper only. When we got home and closed those doors, she did nothing she told my mom she was going to do just the opposite.

I started classes at Forest Park Community College but decided to go to the NFL. I got an invitation to go to the draft, the free agent camp. Both Green Bay and the Chiefs picked me up

The Washington Red Skins recruited my neighbor, Ron Stokes that lived down the street. We were both very excited.

I started the Green Bay training camp but unfortunately injured my hamstring and was placed on reserve. I wasn't ready for the season so I was placed on a wait list. After that I decided to become a police officer. I chose police work instead of football only because of the injury.

Moses Evans had been a cop for years. He was the preacher in the church where I attended and a full time police officer.

He would always say, "If you want to be a cop, let me know. I'll put in a good word for you."

"No thanks, I want to play football."

(Super Bowl Commercial years later)

But he kept on me, persistently. "We're still waiting on you."

Eventually, under my own duress, I had to make money since I had gotten married and had kids. I finally put in an application.

The police force called me. And the show began.

I started dreaming about getting bigger in bodybuilding. I was competing and winning titles. My first title was Mr. Teenage St. Louis. I was fifteen. Then I became Mr. Vic Tanny, Mr. Min America, Mr. All America, Mr. Heart of America, Mr. Ohio Valley, Mr. Missouri, Mr. Mid-West...so many different misters. I competed during high school and I started kickboxing with the St. Louis Whirlwinds. I was a kick boxer, martial arts and hand-to-hand. I still competed when I was a detective and policeman. At this time, they had the Police Olympics annually. I won every single year. Five years straight I won and was the most valuable lifter in all the competitions.

Unfortunately, I was the only African American male in the competition. Everyone else was of another race. I was loved and respected but they hated to see me coming 'cause I would win!

At Forest Park Community College I studied criminology and psychology, as a lot of successful kids come from hard times via the ghetto. Once they apply themselves they can achieve their dreams become doctors... and have the ability to become great at whatever they do. The NBA and NFL are full of kids who came out of challenging environments.

Community College was my opportunity out of my environment and that experience leads me toward law enforcement.

OSCAR "BIG O" DILLON
SAG/AFTRA

" What you lack in talent can be made up with desire, hustle and giving 110% all the time"

Don Zimmer

Chapter 3
I lost My Brother
to the Streets

Donald Erwin Dillon

I was a cop now, but I was even more determined to compete in the World Power Championships in the AAU. My little brother came up to me a couple days before, when I pulled up to my mother's house. He grabbed me and hugged me, which he almost never did.

I said, "What's up with you, everything alright?"

He said, "All my friends tell me that I'm lucky to have a brother like you."

I won Mr. St. Louis, Mr. Missouri, Mr. USA, Mr. Heart of America - I got a lot of titles and this is what drove me to LA. Anyway, my little brother was a year and a half younger than me. The next day, ironically, I competed. I won. It was in the papers, with my name and a write up and all that. I get off from work as a police officer and the phone rings. I had to go back to court later but it was around 7:00 am. But the phone was ringing and ringing and it won't stop ringing. I was trying to get in a nap.

I answered it and said, "Is this about court?"

It was my aunt. She said, "Jerry..."

By the way, Jerry's a nickname my aunt gave me 'cause I act like Jerry Lewis. I'm the silly kid around family functions. I was just funny! She said that she was going to start calling me Jerry Lewis if I didn't stop. I didn't. Everyone started calling me Jerry.

I picked up the phone and she said, "You've got to get over here right now."

I thought someone was sick in my family. I said, "What's wrong?"

She said, "Come now, as fast as you can."

I could feel it. I heard someone screaming in the background. I didn't know who it was. I didn't know if it was my mother, my sister. It was like a death scream in the background

I said, "I'm on my way."

I grabbed my car keys, jumped in the car and ran every red light to my mother's house. I get there and cars are everywhere. There's a fire truck, police cars. There is no party going on at my mom's house. Something… it can't be my mom. My mom didn't die. I walk up to the door, real slow. I'm thinking, breathing…It's different on the street, this is family. I said to myself, handle yourself Oscar, everyone else is lost right now so I need to be strong. I walk in the door and I've got cousins and family rolling and crying. My dad walks out of the bedroom to the front. He looks at me. I stare it him and we pause, maybe 30 seconds.

He said, "It's your brother."

"My brother what?" "Someone shot him." I got this chill. "You mean Donald, my little brother?"

"Yeah."

"Is he?"

"He's not here anymore."

I said, "Aww don't tell me that, don't tell me that. Do not tell me that."

"I'm telling you. It's real."

"Where is he, where's his body. I want to see his body."

"Stay cool now. He's over at the hospital in the morgue."

I didn't know that. I thought he was in a room. Maybe his body was still a little warm or something. I fly over there, and I drive my dad with me another 100 miles per hour trip. I walk in the hospital and all the people in the hospital know me because I brought so many cases there. I know the nurses and the doctors. I walk in and they meet me at the door. They knew I was coming.

The door opened and I said, "Where's my brother?"

"He's in the morgue."

He didn't make it to a hospital bed. He went directly to the morgue pending investigation, preventing the body from deteriorating. I slowly walk to the morgue. It's a metal refrigerator type of door. I take the handle and open it. I see his toe tag. I recognized his feet and his legs. I peel the cover back slowly. I look. He's got a look on his face, a pained look on his face. He had a lot of holes in his face from all the bullets that hit him. When your heart stops, whatever position your body's in, that's where it locks. Imagine you're fighting and you get stabbed in the throat and you're fighting and fighting and you die. You land with your arms like that; with your mouth open and your eyes open. That's how they found him. The last heartbeat creates a stigma of the body and it becomes rigid.

I was pissed, "I'm going to find out who did this."

My brother worked on an assembly line in a plant. One of his positions, he was standing next to a girl. I later found out that she was a crack addict. She was hitting on him. But she also had a boyfriend living with her at home who was a known repeat offender, a criminal. For some reason she was attracted to my brother.

She kept taunting him, "Hey baby, hey baby."

He would say, "Would you stop?"

She took offense one day.

He'd say, "Leave me alone. I'm not interested. I'm doing my work."

She went home at the end of the day and told her boyfriend/suspect that my brother threatened her, which was a lie.

The suspect said, "What, he said what?"

The suspect called his partner in crime and said, "Come over here and bring the stuff."

Two guys went to my brother's job. They waited for him to get to work. They arrived before him. They planned that when he clocks in he has to have his back to the door. They were there hiding already. One was behind the door and the other behind the bushes. They wanted to ambush him. My brother thinks no big deal about it. He's just going to work. As soon as he gets his time card, there were people everywhere. They shot him in the back six times. As he simultaneously turns, they shot him in his face and his brain. As my brother fell, they shot him in his heart and finished him. Then they walked away. I don't think it was retaliation regarding me. I think it was the girl and the jealous drug addict boyfriend. The guy had a violent history. He was that kind of person.

I went on a mission to get him. He was leaving town. They lived in a four bedroom flat. They're out at night and they sleep between 3:00 and 6:00 or 7:00. Knowing that, I figured that they needed to get rest sometime. We're going to hit those spots. I get there and his mother opens the door. I could tell that she was lying.

I said, "Mam, I'm Detective Dillon. We're looking for your son. Is he in?"

"No he's not in."

In the mind of a police officer you have to move fast and skillfully to catch suspects.

Some other investigators that were there earlier searching for the suspect went to the door and said, "You see that guy? He's is a top detective and your son murdered his brother, and if your son wants a deal he should turn himself over to us."

They told his mother that. She lied again.

The guys came back to us and said, "Dillon, he's all yours. We tried."

I ran it. He went to Detroit. Bottom line, fast forward, I got close and then I lost him.

I finally found out that he died years later from a drug overdose. And that was that. The girl that created the whole mess, I heard that someone killed her. It had nothing to do with me, it was drugs.

It's real life. For some reason, if someone wants you because of drugs, if someone wants you dead, they want to jack you and they're desperate and they know you.

You can't trust anybody. It's a whole other world.

"Greatness does not come without adversity, pain, vision and relentlessness as well as a personal relationship with God."

Oscar "Big O" Dillon

Chapter 4
Detective Dillon

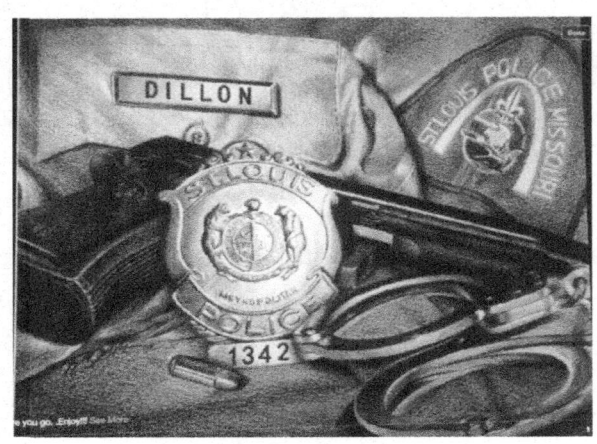

In the meantime, the woman I was married too and I were separated several times, trying to make the marriage work. She said she wanted a girl.

I said, "A girl? We have a boy already!"

She said, "If you can't give me a girl, what good are you?"

I said, "Are you kidding me?"

After a separation, she called me up and gave me something that I asked for but she would never do. That motivated my mind. She opened the door up with a negligee on with some heels and that was my weakness.

Boys lose their minds, and we ended up being intimate again.

When it was all over I said, "I have not seen you in months. You call me up to come over here and we get tangled up. Where is this going? You're still the same."

She said, "No I want you back."

I said, "No, there's no way. You're the same person. No way!"

We split again and weeks later she tells me, "I'm pregnant."

When I was young, if I looked at you you'd get pregnant. Don't look at me if I'm seventeen or eighteen if you don't want to get pregnant! I was that virile because I was popping vitamins every day, working out… my body was just strong. I was like a baby machine.

We separated three or four different times-months at a time, trying again. It doesn't work between us.

My mom pleaded, "Honey, try to make it work. You've got kids. Do what you have to do."

The final straw, I'm in my police car. There's a riot going on in the north end of town. No police officers available. I get called over there. It spills into a party, a nightclub. Bodies are on the sidewalk.

I roll up and say on the radio, "Send me some cars from somewhere. I got bodies on the side walk."

People are running around yelling who shot who? I see my wife, who I'm still legally married to, standing next to a little DJ with his arm around her and his coat around her. They were all hugged up. I pulled up, it was out of my district and ironically it was meant to be that I catch her. I usually worked nights and I'm thinking she was home with the kids. She left the kids at her mother's house and she went to party. I was at work.

When I got out of the car, the guy goes, "Damn, that's a big f…ing cop!"

My wife says, "Oh my God, that's my husband!"

He took his arm away and said, "That's your husband? I thought you weren't with him anymore. I didn't know he was that big!"

She said, "Yeah we are."

I responded quickly, "No, no, no... we aren't together, especially not now. You guys look good together. I'm not mad. Put your arm back around her. I just came to investigate this case and honey, you'll be home before me 'cause I have paper work to do, but pack my bags so I can get the hell out."

He whimpered, "I ain't got nothing to do with this, man."

I said, "It's OK dude. I am not going to do anything to you it's her. If you want a divorce it's done. If you want it you file for it 'cause you mentioned it. File for it, I won't fight it and it's done."

That's what she did. She divorced me of her own free will. I think it was 1979. We were married five years. I didn't contest it. Gave her the house, credit cards...I said I don't care. I'm just out. I said I will always take care of my kids.

For years she apologized and said, "I want my husband back. My kids need their father back so they don't turn to the street."

My boys had grown angry with me. My kids grew up thinking my dad left me. I asked my son later on, ten or fifteen years later, "Why did you distance yourself from me? All my phone calls..."

He said, "First of all, it took me years to figure out that my mom was not right towards you. I'm a man now and I see how she treated you 'cause she treats me the same way. She controls me. She won't get her drivers license. She makes me drive her everywhere. She talks to me like she's trying to run my business. I know how she was with you."

I said, "I tried to tell you that but you were too young to understand. I lost all those years with you but you're a man now and you see the truth."

"I see the truth Dad, I'm sorry. I know you tried to fight for your marriage. She told me you didn't. She said she caught you cheating.

My daughter was not happy about the divorce but there was nothing I could do.

Subsequently once I qualified to become a pro body builder, I had gotten involved in this shoot out while I was a detective and off duty. It turned me off about blood and violence and guns- taking life. (I realized at that time I would rather save life than take life.) Right after the shooting my mom saw me on TV and it said Breaking News. There I am, standing over two dead bodies and all bloody. She called the police station. She thought I was shot because I was covered in the suspects' blood. She immediately called the police station.

"Is my son OK? Is he shot? Did Detective Dillon get shot?"

My dad got home and reassured her, "No honey, he's OK. He stopped the bad guys"

In the midst of all that the divorce was being finalized. I just wanted a new life. I got tired of it because where I was working it was strictly blood and guts all day long. It's every call. People don't understand how difficult a cop's job is everyday.

Most of the cops in business districts, they handle burglaries, car theft, maybe a robbery once in a while. But I remember a call I got. This young teenage girl had just stabbed the hell out of her own brother over a bologna sandwich. This is a true story. A kid on Christmas Day got into it with his sister over the last bologna sandwich 'cause they had no more food. They got into it when the momma was at the aunt's house. She took a butcher knife and stabbed her brother in the chest twice and ki led him on Christmas Day. They were both only teenagers. I got the call. I get there as one-man unit, by myself. I walk in and I see the blood oozing toward the exit. I follow the blood trail. I see the girl in the corner in shock. The bloody knife is over to the side and her hands are all bloody as well. The boy is on the floor. I see he's gone.

I looked at her and said, "Did you do this?"

"I'm sorry, I'm sorry..."

"Is that your brother?"

"Yeah."

"Why? That sandwich was the cause of it?"

"That's all we had. He tried to take it from me and we got in a fight. I just grabbed the knife cause he punched me and I ..."

People don't know. These kids in the ghetto that don't get love with no parents, they're like a ticking time bomb ready to explode at any given moment. Somebody needs to wrap their arms around them and let them know it's going to be OK. I care. I'm sorry your daddy isn't here, no he's in prison. You don't know him. But guess what son; I can be your daddy for right now. You want to talk? Let's talk. Give me a hug. When I walk into a room I say, guess what guys, Daddy's home. Who mad here? What 'cha all mad about today? Talk to me. Gotta break it down to their level. Gotta do the street thing. Can't come across all proper like an insurance man with a tie and all that. You got to learn how to get their attention and I know how to do that.

Everything that I was pissed off about, I channeled into my workouts and into the gym. I built this body from all the pain I have endured. I then became a Batman fighter, a Conan fighter, I help people. People want to know more about me. I bet some of you want to know how I got this way, huh?

Some boys say, "How do you build a body like that?"

I'll tell you how. You've got to flip your mind around and say I WANT TO BE. You have to focus on where you want to be not where you've been. You take where you've been and drive it to where you want to be. You've got to do it within yourself. You've got to make up your mind that you're tired of your situation.

I want somebody to get to these kids before they get there. They need somebody to hug them, somebody to help them. They need a daddy to help them. Their daddy's is in prison. Somebody's got to catch them. I like to talk to kids. You gotta talk to them like you're in the street. You want to curse I can bring it. Just breathe, relax man. Don't try to Kojak me. I can go there man but I'd rather hug you. Just pretend I'm your Dad for a minute. The Dad you never had. I was pissed just like you. I was angry, I was mad. I didn't trust anybody. I didn't care about nobody. Maybe you should just start pumping iron.

They'd ask, "How'd you get like that? How'd you get like that?"

I said, "When I was you, I became this."

I can't do nothing unless I change what I'm doing, how I'm living. Change in your life only happens when you decide within yourself that you had enough of the stuff, the crap, everything going wrong. You can make it right. I'm going to tell you how to do it. Ya'll listen to me. I said ya'll that's right. Ya'll. Ya dig? Ya'll. You understand what that means. That's from the hood. Most of us come from the hood. You don't have to be Black. Some are White from the hood. It's just a White hood. Ya'll just don't realize it. There was a place when I was a cop called Deigo Hill. They were red necks. They'd stab each other, cut each other up twenty-five times a day. White, Black people are the same.

Unfortunately, law enforcement focuses on Black hoods. They don't talk about the White hoods 'cause it's embarrassing if they go to a White family and they act like these Black people. Some of ya'll crazy, too. It ain't just Black people. Let's be real. That's right, White trash people. Can't say "What's up White trash?" You might get slapped or cut. Or shot. On a joking sense- not with a 9 milliliter but with an Uzi gun. Let me tell you something. Black people are crazy but White people are crazier. When you go crazy, you kill a whole lot of people. We don't do that. We just kill each other. You piss me off I just come shoot you in the face. It's over with. You, your cousin, your brother are gang members. I'll just spray all ya'll. Most of your child molesters, what color are they?

Criminals come in all colors and flavors. So let me tell you something. It's not about color. It's about stupidity, and it comes in all flavors. There are some Chinese fools out there too, and Japanese. All kinds of crazy stuff I've seen.

I would get my man but what changed things is that I got tired of shooting people.

Many times just before they died some would say,

"I'm sorry. I was trying to get money to feed my kids."

Sometimes they were kids.

I'd say, "So why'd you shoot at me? Why'd you try to kill me?"

"I'm sorry officer. I really didn't want to. It was just a reflex."

Like I said, sometimes they were kids, like a 17-year-old kid who I didn't know was 17 climbing out a ladies window in the daytime on a burglary. He shot at me and I was just coming into work. I get the call, burglary in progress. I arrive at the house and this kid is climbing out the window and he has a gun in his hands.

I yell, "Police. Stop. Halt. Stop!"

He turns and looks at me and starts shooting so I had to return fire.

I yell, " Shots fired! Shots fired!"

I knew I hit him because of the way he stumbled. He wasn't shot in a kill zone, as we call it. He ran. He left a blood trail and we brought in K9 unit. We look for him and we found him a half a block away behind a trashcan. He expired. Now I've got to go home. This is one episode of one day. I do this all day long. I go home at the end of the day and try to get some sleep. All these flashbacks are killing me. I had nightmares, almost like a sense PTSD.

Later on, fast forward, after working in this division, my dad called and said I'm taking a vacation. We can go fishing. We'll take a week. Come by the shop. When I get to the shop, there are people everywhere. There's Church's Chicken, there's always a liquor store, looks like the ghetto. I was standing in front of the shop and we were talking. We're talking about fishing and I said that'd be great dad. All of a sudden, boom...boom…boom…

I grab my dad, and barked, "Oh shoot dad, he just shot those two guys."

My dad grabbed my hand and begged, "Don't get involved."

I had my gun strapped on my ankle.

I directed my dad, "Dad, do me a favor. Go call and say there's an officer involved in a homicide right now. Send back up immediately. Do not shoot the undercover officer. He's wearing a grey shirt and jeans."

You know, that can happen, friendly fire. I was off duty. After shooting that guy… it happens so fast, within a minute… I come back and there's another guy with a gun that I bump into. He points the gun at me and as soon as he raises his hand to point the gun at me I said 'police' and wrapped around him in a Judo hold and took the gun. When I took it he had his finger on the trigger. As I spun him, the bullet went through my shirt. It went right next to my heart. It scraped the skin but no entry. We wrestled for a minute. I'm getting the best of him. I had to pull back. He had his gun up in the air. He was on PCP. I leaned back for a hip shot and I hit him in his chest. That just pissed him off. Blood shot like a water hose all over me. He fell to the ground and I shot him one more time. I'm trying to keep the muzzle pointed this way, away from me and other people. I hit him one more time with the bunt of my gun and split his head. He was like an animal. He tried to bite me. I hit him one more time and he finally dropped. I fell on top of him and now things are over. I had both guns in my hands, his and mine. People are screaming. It was like a movie. Two hundred people were watching this. They were running, freaking out and crying.

"You saved our lives!"

I'm standing there with his gun in my hand, blood all over me and standing over his body. People were clapping like it was part of a movie. I'm thinking- wow this just happened. My dad runs over to me and grabs me.

He cried out, "Oh my God, you're hit!"

"No dad, the bullet tore my shirt."

"Oh my God, you scared the Beh-Jesus out of me! Never do that again!"

"Dad, this is what I do every day! It's just another walk in the park. I made it through another one."

I probably had PTSD right then. I had lost a couple partners. I saw one of my partners blow his brains out in front of me because he was stressed over his financial situation and home life. I couldn't believe it. I think I survived all of that because I would work out and I had God with me. Even though they were bad guys, the last two shootings I saw their brains all over the ground. I had to look around to get a perspective on the time frame of the shootings. I went through Internal Affairs (IA).

They said, "Dillon, it was a clean shooting. Go see Dr. Cooper and make sure you're OK. Just get it off your chest. It's protocol after a shooting. Just get your check-up. You got a week off and when you come back you won't be in the same location."

Shortly after that, I was in my detective unit with my partner and we got another call for several shootings. When I got there I said, "This just doesn't end. After this, I'm done."

"What do you mean you're done? We need you here."

"I'm not joking. I'm really done after this."

If you keep going back into the same area, you will have flashbacks. If you're a good cop and you hesitate, then you're gone. It's a thin line, a catch 22, staying alive in those circumstances.

I was a cop for ten long years.

After that shooting, that's what prompted me to turn in my badge. After that shooting, maybe a week later, I went into work and I went into the captain's office.

He said, "Dillon, what's up? You got a look on your face, what's going on?"

I took my badge off. I announced, "I'm done."

Captain, "What?"

"I'm done. I need something different."

Just before that, I had my doctor's appointment. I remember him, Dr. Cooper.

Dr. Cooper said, "Dillon, sit down. I have to ask you something. As a father... you're not just a cop. You are special. You have a lot of great skills. You're a musician. You're all over the place doing great things. You're too big for this place. We've got nothing for you. What if you get shot in the back by some junkie on the corner?"

I looked at him, "You know, it could happen. I don't think about it. But you can't see everything."

He said, "If I were you, I'm just going to offer my opinion because I love you so much. I would get the hell out."

I said, "What do you mean?"

He persisted, "If you want to continue being a cop, go to Hawaii or California. LAPD- they make twice what you guys are making. It's a bigger police department."

I lived in that world. I was there. I watched cops cover up and get covered up. But you couldn't ride with me or be in the car with me and do that. I wouldn't let you. I treat people all the same. You're either wrong or you're right. The punishment will fit the crime. If you get pulled over, keep your hands on the steering wheel. Then put your camera on immediately.

As being an ex-police officer I would live to give you some advice, if you are pulled over on how to handle the situation. The moment you see the cop with the lights on in case it's you they're going to pull over. Point the camera toward you and the door. Let it run. When he walks to the car, the camera is rolling if he says anything wrong or inappropriate. A lot of cops forget about the cameras. Cameras are new, basically.

Anyway, after ten years with the police force in St. Louis, I was thinking of going to FBI training I was still a competitive bodybuilder. I thought I could train for Mr. America and hang out with Arnold and those guys.

I was 27 or 28 and I said, "Dillon, you're still young! You got your whole life ahead of you. Do something big with yourself."

After all these shootings, I declared, "I'm tired of all this blood and guts and shooting.

At that time I couldn't sleep so after consulting with my doctor he recommended that I not only leave the Police force but get out of St Louis all together.

I was sitting up in bed and I said I'm getting too old for this shit! I told myself I am going to California- Los Angeles.

Around that time I had applied for a position with the Federal government and they offered me the job. I didn't take it because after thinking about it I didn't want to become to be an FBI agent. I knew my career in police work was behind me.

Before I came to California, I got a phone call. I was a detective at the time in the Tactical Anti-Crime Team (TACT). I was on a Special Forces team selected by the mayor and the Chief of Police. I had a record of going after bad guys.

It was me and about ten other guys were in the same group. The mayor and the chief handpicked us. We were an elite group of police officers who were amazing and would go after the bad guys who could not be caught. Since I grew up in the ghetto, I know how bad guys think. I told them, no more uniform for me.

Chief said, "You're going in plain clothes, or in disguise.

You're going undercover or wired in the trunk of a car. And I want this killer caught.

You guys are my boys. Go under cover, go in disguise, be a cab driver, do whatever you got to do. You're out. You're moving. You're seen."

I said, "OK, give me a profile."

Chief said, "Go find my man."

I got my man 99% of the time.

I was known as super cop. I was like Kojak. I had a suit, a trench coat and a great big gun.

The characters I would later play in movies I lived in real life.

I retired from the police force then proceeded on my journey to California.

OSCAR DILLON
9 YEAR ST. LOUIS DETECTIVE

"The ultimate measure of a man is not where he stands in moments of comfort and convenience, but where he stands at times of challenge and controversy."

Martin Luther King Jr.

Chapter 5
Moving To LA
Experiencing Hollywood

When I first got to LA, I did security for the Red Onion. That's what fed me for a couple months. I was sleeping in my car up near Universal Studios, before I got the job there.

Then I met this big time producer. He met me at a gas station when I was brand new in town.

He said, "My you got some kind of body on you. Who are you?"

He knew I wasn't from here. I had Missouri plates on.

I said, "Who are you?"

"Who am I? I'm somebody who can whip your ass."

He was joking. He was testing me. I'm a big guy with muscles. He was really testing me.

I laughed, "You're very funny but you might kick my ass 'cause I'm kind of tired."

He laughed and got out of his car and handed me his card.

"I'm a big time producer and manager. I'd love to manage you. Come to my Hollywood office so we can talk. Bring your photos and whatever you have."

I kind of got excited. I showed up. We talked. He got all my information and said he was going to get me some work. Blah blah blah….then during the second meeting he started touching me.

"Wow, what do you do with all this muscle here? You've got some amazing legs. What's it take for a man like you? How much are you worth?"

"I'm worth millions man."

"No, no, no everyman has a price. What's your price?"

I said, "I'm out. See you later. Don't bother calling!"

Once an older man touches you, it's confusing. You think it felt great. Now you're coming back for a hundred thousand dollars instead of sixty thousand. You start to like this and now you like men. Most of the older gay guys go to younger good-looking boys 'cause they're easily turned out with green backs. You can get a brand new BMW and never catch another bus again. Not for me!

In the very beginning of my career I was introduced to a different side of Hollywood and had a lot of crazy experiences.

A woman who claimed to be Arnold Swartzenegger's ex-girlfriend had some stock in a bank with another lady in Santa Monica. I was at a meeting and I met her. They were coming on to me but mainly the blond one said, "No, he's mine."

She questioned me, "You're starting to act some?"

"Yeah, a few things." "I'm going to an awards ceremony tonight and I'd like to take you with me.

I'll send a limo to come get you.

I'll send you to a place to get a tuxedo. They're waiting for you. Whatever you need just let me know. "

"What're you talking about?"

"I will buy a condo for you. I'd like to buy a new corvette for you, too."

She had money and I guess she was a low-key producer.

The girlfriend comes behind her back and says, "Why don't I buy you a corvette? She doesn't love you. She just wants your body, that's all. I like who you are. I want a relationship with you."

Both of them were twenty years older than me. They became very competitive with each other to get my attention.

I said, "Does she know you're hitting on me behind her back?"

"No we can't tell her. Once we buy the corvette then of course she'll know. I don't care about her."

I'm new in town but this is interesting and all different to me.

Is this how it is out here? I had little things in St. Louis but this is huge! Every time I take a step someone is after me for sex. The bottom line is I eased out of that one.

I pissed off the blond but didn't really care.

I said, "I don't want the corvette from you and I don't want the condo. Stop, be my friend, be real 'cause I can't handle all this crap. You guys are playing around with me for sex and I'm not into that."

They didn't want anything to do with me after that and moved on. This was just before the Conan Show when I first arrived in town.

What I did get excited about was the fact I got a chance to work out with Arnold at the beach- the famous Venice Beach where all the body builders hung out. It was insane to think I finally got my chance to work out with Arnold and Lou Ferrigno was there. We were lifting 700 pounds. Wow as a teenager that was my dream.

" If you are working on something exciting that you really care about, you don't have to be pushed. The vision pulls you"

Steve Jobs

Chapter 6

Conan the Barbarian Show:

A Sword and Sorcery

Like I said, I started working at the Red Onion on Wilshire in Los Angeles when I arrived in LA. It was a club and I was coordinating the people who were allowed to come in. I'm at work, I'm wearing a suit like a businessman and I'm standing in the lobby. I was about 270 lbs. and everyone was looking at me like who's that guy. I felt a tap on my shoulder. I thought it was a kid 'cause they were short.

I turned around and said, "Hi, grandma."

She was about 4'7", tiny.

"Can I help you?"

Her husband studied me, "You got some kind of body under that coat man. Your muscles are bulging out of the suit. Who are you?"

"Well, I'm head of security."

"You don't belong here doing this."

I smiled, "You guys are very funny. What should I be doing then?"

"You should be in movies!"

"Really, I hadn't thought about it but I'll take your word if you say so."

She came around and pointed her finger at me and said, "You aught to be doing that show that they're casting for at Universal Studios called Conan the Barbarian based on the movie.

I think tomorrow is the last day."

I guess it was on TV and it was a cattle call.

I said, "Where's Universal Studios at."

"It's down at the 101 and Lankershim Blvd. You'll find it."

"I'm new in town. I don't know where things are at yet."

I was working still but that night I kept thinking about it. What'd I come here for? Certainly not to be head of security in a club! That's beneath my dignity! They were only paying me fifteen bucks an hour or something like that.

Hmm, when I drove here in my corvette in the middle of the night like a mad man all I knew was that I was going to Los Angeles. I didn't know anyone. I just knew I needed to get to Los Angeles and get ready to compete. I took a chance.

As I'm ready to drive out of my hometown, my family was in the front yard and they argued with me, "You lost your mind. Are you just going to leave your entire family like that? All of a sudden you quit the police department?"

I said, "Don't worry about it. I just need a jacket and a couple pairs of tennis shoes. I'll put them in my corvette.

I just bought new furniture but you can have it. You can have whatever is in my condo. I'll pay the bill to move everything."

My mom said, "You've really lost your mind."

"No, ma, I'm really leaving. Seriously."

"You can't do that!"

My dad actually sided with me, "Honey, he's a grown man and sometimes a man needs to spread his wings. He knows where home is. Let him go. I'm sure he knows what he's doing. We're going to miss him, yes, but he knows where home is. Don't you son?"

"Yes Dad, I know where home is."

"Mom, it's not about me wanting to be away from you. I'm tired of you sitting at the kitchen table with bills all over the table and crying. I ask you what's wrong and you say nothing."

My dad said, "We're trying."

"I know that you can't pay these bills and you're still struggling. You guys suffer in secret and think we don't know about it. I'm your son, I'm your oldest son and I see through this stuff. I'm so sick and tired like when we were kids seeing you guys struggling from week to week. Somebody's got to do something to change this. Guess what, it's me. I'm going to go.

When I had been back home, Dr. Cooper said, "Dillon, get out of here. Go somewhere. You're worth more than this town has to offer you."

Back to the audition at Universal Studios, I sat on my bed and rocked while I was thinking. You know how you really think about something? Your adrenaline is pumping. Just go! I kept hearing this voice. You don't have to figure things out. Just go. You don't know what to expect. Just go. I couldn't sleep.

Then I said screw it. I grabbed my gym bag. Threw some stuff in there. I went up to Barham and saw all these body builders. It was like an a sea of body builders. Holy Jesus!

I parked the car and signed up. I got a tag like cattle. I'm standing there and there were like two hundred guys in front of me. I'm trying to see the front and it isn't moving fast. It was hot outside, too. I said this sucks. A parking attendant came around.

I asked, "How long has this been going on?"

"About a week or two."

I said, "I'm outa here man. I am not going to do this."

I grabbed my bag and walked away.

"I am not doing this. I'm not going to stand in line like this. I'm better than this."

I see guys going by saying, F…I'm better than him, what'd they cut me for?

They were cutting guys right away. Some guys were so big and steroided out that they couldn't move. They needed people who could move, fight, agile…not just big. I remember Tony Carrol had that monster walk.

"Dude, I saw you running here man. You're like a deer. You move fast. I'm telling you something man, I got a good feeling about you. I don't know you but I've been seeing the guys coming here. I wouldn't leave if I was you. I'm going to tell you a secret. There's another line way down there. It's shorter. A lot of guys don't know that. Go in that line and wait it out. I got a feeling they are going to like you."

I went to the new line. Stood back in line and put my tag back on. They called me in and lined up people based on looks first. I was in the last group that they kept. They said when you come up tell me who you are, where you come from, if you have a specialty in martial arts or whatever. We had to bring weapons if we had a specialty. Bernie Pok and Al Leong had their martial arts weapons, sword and quando. They were amazing. I did a couple things like a diving roll and I had some nun-chucks I think. I did some katas and other martial arts things. I think I did a backward flip at 270 pounds and landed real soft like a cat. I was an athlete. I had to run with Red Sonja over my shoulder up the stairs five, six, eight times a day. We had a physical show which kept us in good shape. It was Gary Goddard, sitting in the front, who said, step up here a little closer.

I said, "What's up? Are you not liking something?"

He stated, "You have an amazing voice."

They were talking about me doing that voice over track. Mike McConaughey ended up doing it.

Remember that line from the show? "Come to me, take the dragon's eye Conan."

He said, "You might be my Taurus Mordor."

I said, "Who's that?"

"He's a character in this show but he's got a James Earl Jones kind of voice."

"See that exit sign over there?"

"Do you want me to leave?"

"No, just go back there and wait for me. Don't say anything to anybody. I'll be there in a couple minutes. Get your stuff and take it with you."

"Oh, OK." Guys asked what happened and I said nothing I'm going to the bathroom.

I was standing at the curtain wondering what's going to happen here. He comes on the other side. He had my file.

"Big O, ex detective, St. Louis police department, body builder, titles, martial arts, you have a great resume and you have a great body. You move like a big cat. Plus you have an amazing voice. Have you ever acted before?"

"I did some modeling, not really acting."

"But you can read obviously."

He shows me the Taurus Mordor lines. He pulled out the script, the original script. I want you to read to me this line right here. 'Conan, take the dragon's eye, come to me barbarian.' I did it but I didn't do it with conviction.

He said, "That's not acting. Be him not you. You're being you. Be him. Be James Earl Jones pissed off. Come out of your stomach with this. Be angry and assertive."

I did it again. He stepped back and said, "You're my man."

He gave me his card and said be here tomorrow morning.

"We got work to do."

We opened that show up in seven weeks. We were sword fighting in the dirt on the top of the hill where City Walk is now. There were several fight choreographers during the ten-year run of the show.

The bosses were constantly changing the fight to keep it fresh and to make it safer. At the end of the first summer, two of the characters were consolidated to cut the budget.

Young Conan also had to play Kobad Shah the warrior, after he grabbed the sword and went down the elevator to magically transform into Big Conan. That's when Conan rose out of the steam and mist to save the day. Zamor was totally cutout and the fight had to be re-choreographed when all the adjustments were made.

In the first round of choreography, Red Sonja had to climb up on his shoulder, dig his eyes out and he would grab her by the hair and throw her on the ground. Big chance to get hurt there, but luckily no one did on that move. There were lots of other injuries though. There were many split fingers and heads when the sword would miss the metal and hit flesh. A true warrior would always spot the target before making contact.

We did a lot of promo when the show opened. Commercials, parades, morning shows, etc. Richie and I took some promo photos with the "Where's the beef?" lady. Pretty funny!

Ok, back to the beginning of my run in the show. Gary the director said, "I want you in this show. I'm not sure where but you're in."

I had just talked to my mother. I had run out of money. I was temporarily sleeping in my car. She urged, "Son, I think it time for you to come back home."

I had called and told her, "Mom, can you just loan me a couple hundred bucks? Just this one time?"

I lost my pension from the police department to the failed marriage.

Mom agreed, "I'm going to send you this but use it to put gas in your car and come home where you belong."

I said alright alright just so she'd send it. But I knew I wasn't going back.

I milked that a little bit, stretched it out. I had the job at the Red Onion. Then we started to get our checks from Conan. I called home and said momma I'm not coming back. I just got hired in Hollywood at Universal Studios on a full time job.

"You did not."

"I did, I did. We're going to be on a five year contract."

"Uh uhhh."

"Yes mom, I'm going to be an actor. I'm not faking. This is real mom."

Then the police department called me, the federal government. They wanted to talk to me. I said that I'm going in a different direction. They wanted me to travel. They wanted me to work with the president. Previously, I had gone to a federal officer-training program and we did some martial arts and other things that agents do when they protect the presidents. We went through a bunch of drills. I had a reputation of being a super cop and they wanted to check out my jacket and my badge. I retired from the police force. That could have been a whole different life.

Richie Brose was the Conan I worked with the most. He gave me so much trouble, but in a fun way. We used to go into restaurants with our costumes on. He was bold.

He'd say, "Oscar, we're going to rock, we're going to bust this restaurant."

I said, "Richie, there's a lot of executives here."

"We're going to have lunch and walk right in the middle of them. We're Conan man."

This was mid-day, in between shows. The show was about 30 minutes. Then we'd go outside for photos with the audience. In the summer, we'd do about 7 shows a day but there'd be three casts so we wouldn't wear out.

There were still many injuries because we used real metal swords, but they weren't sharp. Sometimes people would duck too late or not at all and get it in the head, like Richie. He got quite a few stitches. We had to stop the show and he'd be taken away in the ambulance. We would wait for another Conan who was on call to show up.

In the winter, there was just one cast a day and maybe only four shows. We had time between shows to get into trouble.

"We're going to show them. This is what you're missing."

We didn't just go in, we made appearances at virtually every restaurant. As we went in people were hovering over us for pictures. It was getting out of control at times!

They'd ask, "What time is your next show? We're going!"

People loved us. I turned around and saw Richie's on top of the table dancing to the music!

I'd say, "Richie, get down from there. We got a show to do. We're going to be late! Let's go!"

We'd jump in the car with our costumes on, get back up the hill at Universal, run through the park, wigs twisted! So many crazy episodes!

After that, I shot a national gladiator commercial for Caesar's Palace, which ran for fifteen, sixteen years. The commercial was running everywhere across the country.

People were calling me, "Big O,I see you all over the place. That Super Bowl commercial you did is Hot!"

'I'd say, "I haven't seen it yet cause I've been busy working."

I'm sure so many people remember the Conan the Barbarian Show live at Universal Studios. We had millions of fans. We forgot. We had regulars who bought a season's pass to come see the show every day.

When the show shut down, there was almost a riot up there. It shouldn't have shut down. I still get emails from guys saying, "Man I played for the NFL and you're the reason why" or "Do you remember me when I was a little boy?"

"You and Richie got me working out. Now I'm a pro body builder."

We were just being friendly with people and we affected their lives. We did what most shows did not do. We would interact with the people after every show. It was good for ratings. We met people from all over the world. I remember when Debbie Allen came to the show. She was standing there with her husband Norm Nixon they took pictures with us. And Steven Spielberg, they were on the lot below us. They'd come up and see a show or two. We had a lot of celebrities come to see the show- Bruce Boxleitner, John Landis.

Many we didn't get a chance to interact with but they were sitting in the front row. Then they were whisked away before we could even say hello. But we also had the regulars and they knew our names. That's not Azura the Axe Man, that's Big O! Little kids would stare at you and look you up and down. Are you real? Are you a cartoon? They had all kinds of crazy questions.

There was a lot of interesting and funny stuff going on at the Conan Castle. I introduced Jack and Leslie. Jack was one of the Conan characters and Leslie was a Red Sonja.

Jack said, "Oscar, tell me about that blonde over there."

I said, "Well, that's Leslie. She's John Wayne's niece."

"She does something to me man. I got a thing about her."

He kept asking about her so I said I'm going to introduce you guys.

I said, "Leslie, come here. Jack, come here."

Jack said, "Don't do that, man."

"I'm just going to introduce you to her. What you do after that, I've done my job."

I called them both over and said, "You guys should talk. There's stuff going on here and I'm tired of being the middle person, so you all talk."

They did their thing, fell in love and got married. Their wedding was a big deal. I was on stage in the wedding with other warriors. It was on the news and they did tons of promo for the show.

Both Jack and Richie had incredible physiques. Our fights were choreographed to a sound track. We had to be at a certain point in the fight according to the music.

As we're slinging our sword and axe I'd say, "Richie slow down! You're ahead of the track!"

Sometimes he would swing this one way and it should have been another! Then he'd have to pause to allow the music catch up! He'd throw some ad-lib moves in 'cause he was way ahead of the track. Richie really knew how to entertain people as a Conan. On the stage, off the stage, women would just love it. When they would see him. He'd toss his hair and turn, and do all kinds of crazy stuff.

Women would go, "Oh My God, what show are you guys in?"

We'd say, "Follow us, we've got a show in fifteen minutes!"

In and around while working at Conan, I was doing security at Wompoppers Restaurant, which later became Tony Roma's restaurant.

The owner asked, "Oscar, you used to be a cop, right? Well Conan is over at 9:00 pm and it gets crazy over here, fights and all. We need security. Would you think about hiring some guys and running security up here?"

I did that during and after the Conan Show. A lot of people didn't know it. I hired like fifteen big guys and trained them. I taught them how to run each station.

Conan the Barbarian was a great show that ran for ten years. I can't get upset about that closing. At the time, a new company purchased Universal Studios and changed the show format. The last I heard, they didn't want to renew the contract for the show. They put in a different show where the Conan Castle once stood. Fans were upset!

We had so many fans that were coming up and complaining. The show can't be over! They were our friends. That's what we'd come to do every day in the summer time. Years later they would go to Universal Studios and be mad that the show had closed.

At the end of the day I am eternally grateful to have been part of such a magnificent show, meet so many amazing people and had a great run.

I realize that nothing lasts forever but this is an experience I will never forget.

"We are all just vehicles on this freeway called life"

Oscar "Big O" Dillon

Chapter 7
My Time
With The
Jacksons

My ex riding partner in the St. Louis Detective Bureau, we called him Mickey but his name was Andrew Davis, was head of security for Motown after leaving the police department a few years before I did. He saw me in a commercial in Los Angeles and tracked me down.

He called me in and stated, "Big O, I need you here with me".

We were really tight. He's like a brother to me.

He said, "Why didn't you tell me you moved to LA?"

I said, "Look, everything happened so fast. I am in California now."

He said, "Tomorrow morning I want your butt here at Motown."

"Where's Motown?"

"In Hollywood, on Hollywood Blvd near Vine."

"Yeah, OK."

"I got some people I want you to meet. You're working with me now. I'm going to tell you right now."

"OK."

I showed up and he greets me in the hallway of Motown. He opens his arms wide and puts them around me. We're standing by the elevator. Dianna Ross passes me by along with another Motown executive, Barry Gordy.

He said, "This is going to be great. Come in this big conference room. Follow me."

I opened the door and who's sitting there- the entire Michael Jackson family. I walk in.

He stated, "Just stand there."

I'm big. They all turn and look at me. Mickey probably gave them the heads up that I was coming. They were getting ready for the Victory Tour.

Michael questioned, "Who's that?"

"This is your man now Michael. This is Big O, my ex-riding partner in the St. Louis police department. He lives here now. He's an actor but guess what. He's working for us now and Michael, I'm going to assign him to you and your family. Trust me, you are in really, really good hands. Trust me. I give him 100% plus!"

Michael smiled, "OK. All right then."

Janet Jackson blinked, "Wow, I feel safe with Big O."

Anyway, I began working with Michael Jackson and they're rehearsing for the Victory Tour. Tito and all of the other Jacksons, we all subsequently became like family.

All the people in the families' inner circle knew the real Michael Jackson the rest of the world doesn't. He simply tried to give kids what he never got, unconditional Love. It was a giveback, because he loved kids, he loved people. He didn't like people who tried to hurt him. He ran away from them 'cause he was shy. But he could give his love to kids 'cause it's always unconditional.

At this point my career started to take a different turn towards acting. I said, "Michael I love ya, I got to go man, got to make some movies."

"Oh Oscar, you're going to leave me?"

"I'm not leaving you. I have to go pursue my dreams now."

When you're a bodyguard, you have no life.

You're their life. If they move, you got to be on it. If they look right, you got to check and make sure things are OK.

If they go left, you got to go check it out first and make sure it's safe. I got to use the bathroom, OK go ahead, I'm coming. I did a lot of advance work for him to make sure he was always safe.

Michael was a lot like Elvis and ironically married Elvis's daughter. Lisa always had a crush on him. Michael married her and wanted to start a family and all that. He was searching for love. He needed a woman who he could love and who could handle his fame and fans

Michael did good things all over the world, stuff for children, We Are The World, We Are the Children- in Africa and all over the world where they loved him like crazy.

I worked with Michael on the Victory Tour in 1984 at the same time I was working at the Conan Show, juggling both.

I worked with Michael for about five years before I took off to work on my own career.

During my time with the Jacksons I found Michael to be a very caring and loving individual, absolutely not what people say and accuse him of being. People who don't really know him.

It was a great experience and the Jacksons will always be in my heart since we were like family.

Michael died in June of 2009 and I feel the world lost a musical genius and a kind man.

I can do all things through Christ who strengthens me.

Philippians 4:13

Chapter 8
An Unbelievable Tragedy

My dad, Oscar Dillon Sr. passed away in 1987.

They didn't tell me my dad was dead; they just… made the phone call and told me that I needed to come home now. This call was made by my aunt and I was not sure what to think.

"Stop whatever you're doing and come home now. We don't know what to do."

"About what? What do you mean come home now? What's going on?"

"Well, it's the family."

"Don't do this to me. I'm too far away. Tell me what's going on. Maybe I can fix it from here."

"No seriously you need to come home now."

Oh, I know what I was doing. I had just shot a Michelob beer commercial at Venice Beach. I shot it that day and then was getting ready to head to my job on the hill.

I went to Dupar's Restaurant to process the phone call in my head, the one on Laurel Canyon and Ventura and I remember sitting there in my seat kind of frozen and lost.

They didn't tell me anything; they didn't want to tell me on the phone. I was thinking about how fast I could get home and what could it be.

I had lost my brother and I knew that tone.

Someone was either close to death or gone. I didn't know who it was. I got on the plane and flew home in a very weird mood with a cloud of uncertainty hanging over my head.

I arrived at my mom's house straight from the airport. There were fire trucks, police cars everywhere the street was totally blocked off.

My dad and I were pretty well known around town. The cops knew my family so they'd hang around my mom's house 'cause of me and my dad and his business and all that. So I get out of the car and it was the longest walk from the street up to the front door. It was like it was slow motion. I open the door and see all these people on the floor just screaming and crying.

My aunt comes out from the bedroom.

She stood there with her hands on her hips and I said, "What?"

"It's your father."

"Where's my dad at?"

I was thinking he was in the hospital.

I said, "You guys are killing me, will you stop it already?"

"Go back to your momma."

Her bedroom was all the way in the back, a long hallway. I'm walking down the hallway slowly and I see people all around the bed. My mom has the covers over her head. The doctor had given her a sedative.

She was shaking and crying, "My baby, my baby, my baby."

I kneeled down and grabbed her hand. She recognized my touch.

"Mom, I'm home."

She screamed like someone was stabbing her with a knife. She grabbed me around the neck so tight I couldn't breathe.

She was screaming, "My baby, oh my God, what am I going to do??"

I knew at that moment it was my father.

Then I smelled burnt stuff, like fire and I said, "What happened?"

He was at the shop and he hired this guy to do some welding. He was Russian. Dad was closing the shop. Minister Childs, who was a guy from the church, asked my dad to reopen the shop to fix his car. He needed it for work the next day. My Dad, being the nice guy that he was, said to my mom who was doing the books in the front office to go ahead and go home. My Mom said she would finish the books for him the next day since she knew he was tired.

He told her, "You go home and get dinner started. I'll be a few minutes. This won't take long."

They only lived about a mile from the shop.

He said to the Russian guy, "You can weld right?"

"Oh yah, I did it all the time in my country." "OK, he's got a crack on the frame so fix it, hopefully, we'll be done in the next half hour to forty five minutes."

The guy went down to the fourth stall and tried to strike the welding torch. He didn't know what he was doing and no one was around him to guide him. My dad was up here fooling around with another car with a gas tank. There was a big oil tank over there filled with combustible stuff.

When the worker my father had recently hired attempted to light the torch the spark hit a gas fume somewhere over there and WHISH there was a small explosion. Now that whole side was on fire. Then BOOM, BOOM,BOOM there was a number of consecutive explosions. So fast, it was an oil fire.

It burned for a week. You can't put oil fires out. They have to burn themselves out. My dad was in this position holding a gas tank. My brother, who just got out of the Marine Corp, was there helping part time. He was in the second stall. The Russian employee who started the explosion was on fire. He ran out. The doors slammed shut. All four doors closed after the explosion. My brother's hands, face and clothes were burning. He sees my dad standing completely engulfed in flames, screaming.

My dad is yelling something but my brother can't make it out, and now my brother's yelling, 'DAD!' He ran to my dad but it's too late. My dad collapsed, it was so bad there were no remains left to put in the coffin. We used a picture of him with his guitar. We made a guitar wreath and then a closed casket with a picture of him sitting on top of the casket. That's all we had.

My brother survived and over time his burns healed. You would never know looking at him. But his mind was never the same since he carried the image of what had happened.

After he found out how it started and found out the facts, my brother wanted to kill the Russian. I convinced my brother not to do it.

He kept saying, "I don't care. It should have been me, not my dad."

The Russian guy left town pretty quickly. He disappeared and we never heard from him again. We lost everything, the business, all the tools, a safe full of money; the families' livelihood was destroyed.

Now I'm there trying to put pieces of the puzzle together. The shop was completely burned, nothing left.

My mom's freaking out, "What am I going to do? I don't know what to do."

She's never been without my dad since she was fourteen years old. Not one day. They were tight and they were happy. They were crazy in love. He was her baby. She never imagined life without him, let alone not being able to say good-bye to him.

When the place was burning, the police and firemen come to the house and said, "Mrs. Dillon, can you come with us please?"

"No because my husband should be here soon. Why are you guys here anyway?"

"It's about your husband."

"What are you talking about?"

"Just come with us please. We'll explain to you on the way."

They get to the car and half way there, I'm sure she's freaking out, you can see the entire block was just flames.

She cried, "Don't tell me, my business."

"Not only that, your husband's in there."

"What? No, he said he's coming home."

"No he's not, he's in that fire. We couldn't get him out. There's nothing left.'

She lost it. They had to rush her to the hospital. Her heart stopped beating. They let her go home figuring the family would watch over her. They gave her a sedative. I walked into that.

I said, "I promise you I won't leave until we get everything worked out." I called back to Los Angeles and asked Charles or maybe Jim Maniachi to cover for me while I was gone from the Conan show.

While I was in St. Louis taking care of everything I had to be strong, I was the rock for my entire family. I wanted to be there for my mom, after all not only did she lose the love of her life, the family income was gone. I had to hide my emotions. That's the cop in me.

When I got back to LA, it hit me like a tons of bricks and I let all of my emotions out. My dad and I were very close he was my **hero.** My dad taught me everything and is the reason I am the man I am today. He was smart, funny with a big heart. My dad was a great musician, excellent singer, an entrepreneur and for five years he was Business Man of the Year.

He sang with his group called The Trumpets, a gospel group. He had a presence about him and everyone loved him.

Once I realized he was gone I felt the pain to my very core. To this day I miss him very much but know his legacy lives on.

" When you have a true authentic personal relationship with God, he will create your pathway"

Oscar "Big O" Dillon

Chapter 9
Working in Movies

1983-2008

OSCAR
DILLON
SAG / AFTRA
ACTOR / STUNTMAN
(BIG O)

My Hollywood movie career was gradually growing. I knew it was not going to be easy but I was determined and beside I was never one to give up.

As my film career continued to thrive I realized that police work was behind me. I knew I did not want to go back to that. People wanted me to but I felt like I'd be backtracking going into that again…shoot, run, chase, and crash. That's why I left in the beginning. So I needed to put the idea to rest that I'd go to the FBI or work for LAPD investigative division.

As soon as I let go of the idea of going back into police work my acting career really started to flourish. I started to be booked for TV and commercials. I landed a recurring role on The Young & the Restless with Victor and Nick Newman for about a year

Then the movies roles started coming in, first B movies then the higher budget movies notice me.

One day I got the call from my agent to go on an interview at Full Moon Entertainment in Glendale. They said they needed a muscular genie kind of character for the leading role. It was with Zachary Ty Brian who had just finished the popular show, *Home Improvement*.

The movie was called *Disney's Magic Island* and I would be playing the role of a magical pirate. The director Sam Irvin offered me the lead role in a movie, but I had to shave my head to accept it.

They said, "We want you for this role but we need you to shave your head. Would you be OK with that? If you can't, we'll have to move on."

"You got the look but your hair is too nice. You have pretty boy hair." "We need you to be menacing. If you shaved your head, you would be perfect."

At first I refused my vanity said," Grrrr.... I don't know, let me think about it."

Later that day I was on the phone with my mom and told her about the situation she said, "Don't you cut your hair. I love your hair."

"Mom, they offered me the role. When I get that money I'm going to send you some to help you out."

" I need to give them a answer since we start shooting next week. We're going to Mexico. We'll be shooting for several months."

"Well then, go ahead and shave it."

I contacted my agent and I said I would do the role.

My whole life changed when I shaved my hair off.

I shaved my head and accepted the role. It was a Disney by Full Moon Entertainment/ Paramount production. Not only did I star in that movie, I was the stunt choreographer, fight choreographer and technical advisor. I did receive screen credits for all of those roles.

Because of the movie I also pierced my ears. When I first started The Conan Show, my ears were not pierced. They had the clip on stuff and I was losing it in the fight and stuff falling off. Finally, I started with one 'cause I was just, argh, it's a girl thing. And guess what, I kept my head bald and I never took these earrings off.

My look became shaped by all of my roles: Conan, gladiator and yes a pirate.

The roles kept rolling in; I shot *Perfect Target* in Mexico with Brian Thompson. I was a federal agent and Brian played the bad guy, a crooked cop.

I did a small role in *Get Shorty*.

The movie *Idlewild* came around 1994. I felt as though I had great character development while shooting this movie. Terrence was hot and I was his buddy, Bobo. This was 2004. Now he's hotter than ever. We were all sitting around talking with Ving Rhames, Faison Love, Terrence Howard, Patti LaBelle, Macy Grey... we're all enjoying lunch.

A short time later I was casted to co-star in a movie called The Wood thanks to casting director Bonnie Timmermann and director Antoine Fuqua. *The Wood* cast included Omar Epps and Taye Diggs

They said, "We need to shoot this thing and we need to make it real. We know you were a cop and we know you got a reputation, so can you set this whole robbery scene up for us?"

I asked, "You want me as technical advisor?"

They said, "Yeah."I made sure that they gave me credit for it.

I got three checks, three separate checks, which I liked.

"Give me a scenario."

They put two cameras on. Bonnie was sitting back there with other producers, an AD, the director and they were sitting at this big table like this. They were watching me and I had a police uniform on. "OK we have three, four suspects...we're going to rob the store. They're going to have a gun. I won't know this when I pull them over. I am going to pull them over once they leave the store. I get distracted. I get a radio call while searching them to go to another scene."

"I want you to make it natural but almost kind of funny, too."

"Ok, I'll do that."

Personally, I thought at the time that the suspects wore Jerry Curl juice, dripping everywhere. You'll see the clip on my site. He's talking to this guy. I pull him over. There's a gun on the floorboard in the back seat that's visible.

Then they're putting the joint out. "Man, put that joint out!" (coughing)

"Step out of the car. Shut up and step out of the car."

My co-partner says, "You heard what he said, step out of the car."

"All of you. Get on the curb over there. Face the wall."

The other guy's crying, "You shut up. I don't want to go to jail man. I'll kick your ass right here in front of these cops."

I said, "Shut the hell up all of ya. Put your hands behind your head and lock your fingers together, everybody. Right now, I don't want to hear another sound. I start to search them. I'm patting down two guys. I say, "What's this?"

He said, "Nothing."

"Ok, get over there."

Then I get the guy with the Jerry Curl. I'm searching him.

"Don't put your hands on me officer."

I give him a dirty look, "What?"

As I'm searching him, I push him against the wall and I'm going up and down his leg, in his waistband like cops do. I search up here and my hand hits his collar. It's filled with Jerry Curl juice. Now I got it all over my hand.

I look in his face and put my hand up to his face, "Really?"

Then I wipe all the stuff on his shirt.

"What chu doing?"

"Shut up!"

It's a funny scene.

Then I say, "You're clean man."

I take the call, robbery in progress. We let them go not realizing these were the suspects.

I said, "All you guys, look at me, get that damn tail light fixed."

We take the call and we take off.

The call came in just before I saw the gun in back seat. It distracted me. Then I told them to get the hell out cause I had to get to this call not realizing the suspects are right here in front of me. Anyway, it's a funny scene. I put all that together and presented it to the director. They just loved it. They showed that film like crazy.

I set it up again in the call back. Bonnie Timmerman and I worked together a few times.

They said create a scene for us. So I do that in their office. I said Bonnie you're there, and I'm just a cop coming in. When I finished the scene I had created they were stunned and excited.

It was so real I got hired on the spot.

They said, 'You got the job. You scared the hell out of me. There's no call back. You're hired.'

Then I did something called *Perfect Weapon* with another martial arts actor with a big name called Jeff Speakman.

I was still competing in bodybuilding. I think Mr. Universe was coming up.

I did a lot of guest spots but I was mostly doing films.

Most of my time was spent on location traveling the world and as a result I speak several foreign languages.

I went to Germany and stayed for about two months where I stared in a show called *Lucas.* I starred in it with Dirk Bach. I have an agent over in Germany named Gird Birkmann. I have a huge fan base there that loves me. What an amazing experience.

Ok, back to the movies. I did Batman. We shot for about three months I think. It was a long period of time. It was for Warner Brothers. I did Batman Forever.

My cousins would say, "See Batman? That's your cousin right there."

"That's my cousin? I want to know him. That man with the muscles, that's my cousin? I want to meet him. I want to show him to all my friends at school!"

Over the last 20-30 years, I've done a lot of movies and TV shows. I've coordinated and stunt coordinated, somewhat directed, created. I've done all of that. I created a whole scene. I did the scene with the robbery, the street scene with the cops and they're rolling up. I created a whole scene for the director. When I walked in for the audition, they said, "Oscar, we want a real life cop to come in and bring intensity to the robbery with the gang members. There's a liquor store with a shop on the street."

While shooting the film Tango and Cash I created a piece for Sylvester Stallone, "Sly, you want to face off with me but we don't want to do anything like anyone else."

We rode bikes together and ate together.

"If I may have a moment, once you take those guys out in the laundry room, all of a sudden you turn, which you're going to do anyway, you pause and I'll be standing there cracking my knuckles. Then I say-Tango, I'm going to tear you a new asshole."

I'm stealing lines so I make sure I'm in the money. I'll get paid for stunts and acting.

Stallone said, "What're you going to do?"

"When you put this guy out, I'm going to come at you ... I'm going to leap at you. My heart is pumping. This is a fast moving scene right? I'm airborne I'm going to aim for your throat. "

He said, "We can't use mats in the shot. It's got to be like this inside the prison."

I said, "We don't need mats. I know what I'm doing."

He said, "But you're going to get hurt."

I said, "No watch me. This is a one-take shot." They loaded up the cameras. Let's get ready. We're going to slow walk it one time then we're going to shoot this puppy."

"Sly, you ready? Let's rock and roll. All you do, you see you and me duck and you spin. I will come over you, as if I have just thrown a punch at you but in the air. I'm going to do a flip and land. You turn and as you turn I turn, too. Then you simultaneously clock me with a big giant stick, a baseball bat in the face. Then throw me into the wash."

Anyway, I created this scene and we did it. One take. We froze-stop, cut.

"Everybody OK? Let's go look at the playback."

We go look at the playback, me and Sly and a couple of the stuntmen. They roll it and Sly says, "Son of a bitch Oscar! Damn bro. You're one bad mother. You OK, man?" I said, "Yeah, I'm fine."

"That was bitchen. That was bitchen!"

He said, "That was amazing!"

He shook my hand and gave me a hug. I made him look good and he appreciated that. Most big guys can't move like me.

"That looked awesome, awesome. Seriously. Good idea Oscar. Ok, now we can get back to work."

Afterward, I did the movie with Carol Burnett and Michael Keaton, that was around 2007/08.

Most of the characters that I do in movies was based on my personal experience being a cop on the streets. You don't have to say anything. I can read your body language from across the street. If you've got a gun or what your intentions are, I can read your body language in thirty seconds to a minute and I can tell exactly what you're getting ready to do.

I was up for another lead role in 2008 before God took me in another direction.

Today I look back on my movie/film/TV career knowing I have been blessed to be in over 35 movie productions and 50 commercials. In addition to the ones I have already mentioned I was in Rising Sun, Another 48 hours, Memorial Day, Fist of honor and on TV in The Closer as well as Family Matters. Plus many, many more.

"We generate fears while we sit. We overcome them by action"

Dr Henry Link

Chapter 10
Diet, Vision, Training & Discipline

I want to share my diet. Also, I want to share that my steroid use was minimal. I didn't use them at all the first twenty-five years or so of my career. I had started working out so young that I was buff before I was a teenager. Most body builders start in their late teens or twenties. Everything I achieved, I did it before I was seventeen. I didn't even know what a steroid was.

I was nervous/respectful of steroids. If I did them like other body builders were doing them, I would have been Mr. Olympia. I was as big as Arnold but I wasn't quite as hard as Arnold. They were all doing so many steroids it was coming out of their ears. I didn't do it to the next level to be an Olympian. I didn't do steroids during The Conan Show. I don't have the temper. I don't like to argue with people. If you want to fight, I'll see you later. I don't have the desire to listen to your garbage and trade words with you. If I stay here, you might swing on me. That would make me hurt you really bad. And I don't want to do that. I'm going to do you a favor and just shake your hand. This is stupid. We're grown men. You hit me. I'll kill you. Who won? What was solved? Nothing.

I worked my ass off. My momma will tell you that boy was crazy and possessed in that basement lifting those weights. I worked out and I ate because I wanted to be big. When my family was eating pork and grits and all that stuff, I'd eat grains and rice and two to three dozen eggs a day. I studied what I should eat. When I was a child, I had all these body building books and magazines. One was Eat to

Win. Another was Train Like a Champion. I had stacks of books that I studied day and night. I read about what the body was made of inside out. I wanted to know, if I'm building my bicep, where does the bicep begin and where does it end so I do full range movement so I don't become muscle bound. I could move because I didn't constrict myself through lifting weights and cause my tendons and ligaments to become coagulated. Then I would have a short reach as a fighter. I was a kick boxer, too.

Tendons and ligaments are made to stretch. If you don't stretch them, they get old and constricted. If you force them to stretch, like a rubber band, they pop. The body is the same way. If you don't use it, it will constrict itself and every time you lift you damage something. You've been sitting there, kicking your legs out instead of working out. There are muscles in there dying. If you don't move them they atrophy. Inside our bodies, they tell us and send us little signals called pain.

Pain is a signal. When you understand that, now you can go inside and understand that my body needs X amount of protein. Then I can change or grow beyond what my mom was feeding me. I eat oatmeal, eggs, wheat toast, wheat pancakes, salads, steak but with the fat cut off. You have to chew it carefully so it doesn't lodge in your colon. Then you have the problem of cancer. Most people don't have a colonoscopy to check for polyps. That's a sign that you may have cancer. You wonder why you're so tired and why you're constipated a lot. The polyps in your colon are trying to get out but they can't. They're stuck. They get trapped and before you know it your colon is almost closed. Instead of it going through, it goes back up. Then you've got a large stomach and you can't breathe. You've got problems. You have to go to have that looked at.

When I was a kid, I had a plan to get of the ghetto. It made me possessed. It drove me past human comprehension. I was a hungry young black kid. My father told me as we were out fishing and having father son conversations while we were waiting for the fish to bite early in the morning.

My dad was amazing, "Son, you know, it's a crazy world we live in. One thing you have to understand, off the bat. You're Black. It's a natural fact. You came into this world and you have one strike against you. It's just the way the world is. Now you have to prove yourself before people have a little bit of respect for you. You can't do it being angry. Be smart. Use this. Get your education. Don't quit school. Most of those guys started school and most of them are dropouts. That's why they're here. These guys are nothing. They're bums. They're dead people walking.

Don't be like that. Not that you're going to be but I'm saying to you- You Be Somebody Great that people will respect as a Blackman.

How do you do that?

You go to school. You get your education. Learn English. Learn to speak well. Don't talk like those other guys- You know man- what's up dog. You know what I'm saying?"

My mom and dad hated that street talk.

They'd say, "What are they saying?"

They both impressed me all the time as a young man. I was working on cars with dad, and learning how to play guitar at five years old. My dad was a country boy and he loved his country music. He came up from Mississippi. They were country boys. My grandmothers both had farms. They grew up on a farm. I spent a lot of my younger years on farms in Jackson, Mississippi. My grandmother used to come get me.

She'd say, "Ok, let's wake up now."

I'd hear the rooster. She'd take me to the chicken coop and pick up some big ol' brown eggs. She'd make a dynamite breakfast. Everything was fresh. I loved going down there and learning things from my grandmother and my grandfather. They taught me how to be a man. If you wanted to go to the store, you had to walk the long dirt road. You had to walk two miles down the road, turn left and walk another mile, get a loaf of bread and turn around and come back. I'd go hunting with my dad and his brothers. I had a shotgun and it was taller than I was. I knew how to handle guns as a boy. I shot all kinds of guns. I was a great shot. We hunted rabbit and squirrel. We'd skin them and gut them open and eat them. Mom would make a great rabbit soup. We brought back a bunch of eggs from the farm and we'd stock up. It saved us a lot of money. There were kids and not enough money. I grew up around a lot of men. My dad had nine siblings and five brothers. They were close and we'd go hunting, fishing, baseball…they were big boys- like football players. I was with them all the time. I went to rehearsals with my dad when his group was practicing.

I could sing and play guitar, too. I was a man before I was a man. I was responsible. My dad could count on me. He'd assign me things almost daily.

He'd say, "I'll be gone for twelve hours. I want you to make sure those cans are out. Get some nails and screws and fix that fence."

He knew I was going to have it done and I'd always do it better than he said. That was important to me.

I wanted him to come to me and say, "Wow, I didn't tell you to do that. You did that one, too? I was going to do that tomorrow."

"They were all falling over. I fixed that one, too."

Mom said, "He's been busy."

"You like it?"

"That's my boy. I'm proud of you." People don't understand. If you tell a boy that they're doing a good job, they will be inclined to do even more."

Nobody really tells them that. They want to please their teachers. You can tell they're going to be something when they get some praise. Nobody loves on them. That doesn't freak them out. Be his friend for a second. Just talk his language for a minute.

Just sit next to him and say, "What's up man?"

When they see that you're not fishing for something, they learn to like you and open up to you.

There's someone up above called God. If you stay connected, he shows favor to some people more than others. He loves everybody, but for some people, when it's time for you to go by natural means or whatever the case may be, it isn't over till God says it's done. I lived that. I'm not a preacher. I'm just going to put it on the table for you as a man from the ghetto. I've been to college. I studied psychology. I'm a decorated cop.

I did some work for some of the biggest stars in the world. I'm an actor. But I'm going to tell you something. See all this that's going on in the world? It's all written in the book we all read. I do not have a forked tongue. I'm going to tell you something straight. All you guys out there- drinking too much, being slick, and abusing your wife… You went to jail once and you aren't stop doing what you're doing and thinking what you're thinking. But, there's something called Karma. Trust me. No one escapes. Not a single one of you escapes what your evil thoughts are or your slick thoughts are because you think no one is looking. You think you have a chance to make a dollar or do whatever. You need to have a relationship with God in some manner today in order for you to have strength enough as a man to keep on being on track. We all have a mind that can trip up if you see an opportunity that's quick and slight and quiet. Many of us can say 'no, I won't do that' but then the next day you say…'who's looking?' Women buy into what we slam on them and they want us to pay for it. You slapped her around. You abuse her. You gave her too much cocaine. You try to sell her. You bring your friends over to sleep with her if they pay you. Some of you guys are sitting right here looking innocent and cute, but you aren't living right man. You're going to pay for that. Trust me. When you pay for it, it won't be a slap on the wrist. You're going to pay for it big. A lot of you guys say this. I heard it too many times.

"I am not scared about dying. Shoot me right now. I don't care about dying."

People like that don't die suddenly. You know what happens? They become disabled. You can't die. You have no arms. You can't even kill yourself. You're lying in the hospital looking at the ceiling and thinking about when you pulled your gun on the police.

Do you know how many people I seen in the hospital roll past me when I was lying in the hospital myself? I talked to them before they died.

I asked them, "Somewhere in there when you come into a place-you got nobody but God, momma gone, family gone and doctors don't really give a damn. They just put you on a whole bunch of drugs and leave. They go play golf. You're hurting like hell. They got nothing to cure the pain that's in you. The nurse is just doing what the doctor told her to do. But you're in a lot of pain and you're saying I just want to die. This hurts so bad I just want to die. But you can't. That's suffering.

Suffering is worse than death, as we know it. But after death that man up there that made you God created you, and he built you to be kind to each other.

Have you ever heard the saying, God don't like ugly? That's the bible. The ugly within you that you think nobody can see 'cause you got it going on like that. All those drugs that you had your boys selling to kids on the corner- one day someone will roll up on you and shoot you, then run you over with their car. Set you on fire. Use acid, because before you die, they want you to suffer.

You don't think that can happen to you?

One tiny mistake and it's not a matter of if but would they, and your day is definitely around the corner. Your date-your date and your date- all of you-you can't hide no more. Because he comes for you when you're in the dark by yourself... Someone call 911. You're going to pay for that. If you rape a child and they put you in prison, they don't like child molesters in there. They'll kill you. They'll beat you to death.

Guess what? You're day's coming.

Whether I scare you or not, I was a freakin' hard-core street cop, man. I could lock you up, straight up. But I'd rather come hug you, man, and say you got a problem.

Speak on it. I'm here to answer your questions. I know you all got questions.

"Take the first step in faith. You don't have to see the whole staircase, just take the first step." -Martin Luther King Jr.

Chapter 11
New Heart
New
Beginnings

God snatched me from **death to life** and placed me back on this earth, for His glory.

Here I am!

Again, I had no choice. I had to give my life up to God and he allowed me to come back from my second code blue. Feels like I've been time traveling, I know I've been seeing my life flash before me, like It's A Wonderful Life or Scrooge without all the ghosts. I've learned a lot. I know I have to start speaking out. This is my new divine purpose in life. I have to share what I've learned. It's not about Big O anymore; it's about Big O, helping others through God.

My stomach was distended. I slept in a recliner for about five years. I had a machine on me, monitoring my heart and I was so distended I couldn't breathe. I couldn't get enough oxygen and the room was spinning. My brain was also spinning and I thought there's no one here and I'm going to die. I had no control of myself at that time.

I was on hydralazine it made me paralyzed, paranoid and I had loss of vision. I got up to go to the bathroom and I couldn't speak, I couldn't move. I felt my heart pounding real fast. I wanted to say something but I couldn't.

I was quietly screaming, "Somebody, somebody around?"

I was at home in the front room by myself. I was on so many drugs and I was hooked up to a life saving medication pump. Everything got blurry. I hit the floor on my knees. Then I went on all fours.

I thought I was shouting, "We got to go! It's time."

Somehow Cindy heard me and came running. We jumped in the car and we drove to Cedars. I admitted myself on November 22nd or 23rd 2014. I checked into the emergency room.

When you enter the hospital, the doctors and nurses are so busy trying to save you, they don't have time to explain to you what is going on.

I prayed every day. I did not want to leave like this. Not like this. I prayed and I worshipped 24/7-every minute of every day. You have to hand your life over to God because you have no control of anything. I had three or four songs that I listened to all the time. I realized at this date in time, that I'm a direct product of Jesus showing me favor to keep me here. There is not a doubt in my mind. It became very clear to me that God was taking me through this miracle of a journey. Here's the problem. When you say that, some people get mad at you because they say why didn't God save my son? I don't know why. When I was born, I really learned to love God as a child. There's no doubt.

When I sang in church as a child, there was a song I used to sing. The song was called Home Going and I sang it for my grandfather's funeral. It was an old folk song that said 'when you hear my home going, don't worry about me, cause I'm just another soldier, on my way home, one thing I know, I've been born again, cause I made preparation on Sunday morning, but when I die, it'll be my time to go, cause I'm fixed up right now, on my way home.'

Another song is- 'I sing because I'm happy, I sing because I'm free, cause God's eyes is on the sparrow, and I know he watches me'. In other words, I'm not going to let you steal my journey. I choose to be happy.

I've always had a relationship with God, ever since I was a little boy. He can trust me to get his truth out. He knows that deep down inside me when the day comes that I become a man and I'll be more assertive and more confident.

God gave me a Barry White voice- people say, "I'd like to see who's got this voice."

This happens everywhere I go, even at Ralph's Supermarket the other day!

I believe that God chooses some of us to remain here for his own reasons that we do not understand. He intends for you to live your life for Him. We are supposed to change our lives and do something for God, not yourself. You know, I've been dead two times, near death many other times as a police officer. I've experienced death. I'm proof. I'm the direct product of the transition that God can do in a human being's life. He created us. We forget that. Yes, you came from your mother's womb but God created man. He is the one thing that many of us have forgotten to give thanks to each and every day. We take it for granted but every five minutes we say 'Oh My God!' OMG! What does that mean? First of all, Oh My God came in from terminology created on the street and social media back when the first cell phone came out. The only people who said it before that was the people in church, in worship and just thankful. Ask any of these people if they prayed lately.

People say that luck was on their side, and I would say, "What did you call that, luck?"

When unexplained things happen in my life I call them miracles not luck. God has the ability to turn tragedies into testimonies.

Did you ever think that you had a purpose for being here beyond that accident? You walked out of that accident with nothing but a scratch and the car was crunched like a can. Why do you think so? Wasn't your time to go? You don't get it, do you? This is what's wrong with most people.

I have a relationship with God because I respect God, the almighty. There's one God and we all call him different things. It is written in the bible. You have your religion. She has hers. You're all referring to the same book. It's just written slightly differently. But it all basically says the same thing. There's one thing for sure. There's only one God. The words that I speak, I won't try to figure it out anymore. When you're shy, you find an excuse not to do things. God gets inside you and creates the event for you through your words. You just surrender and it flows. Even if you've coordinated what you're going to say to a degree, in the midst of it all greatness is happening. If there is anything that is happening right now, you should not be wasting your life. The world is never going to be the same, but we do have hope. If you lose your mind, basically your body is going to follow.

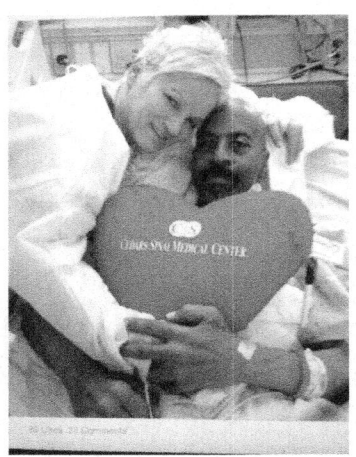

In about 2011, I was told that I needed a new heart. I was in denial for a couple of years. I didn't want to hear that. I believed God was going to fix what I had but mine was damaged and oversized. So Dr. Moraguchi got really mad at me because I would not check myself into the hospital and he walked out on me. I was being stubborn. He wanted me to check myself in because he thought I wouldn't be alive.

He actually yelled at me, "You're going to die and you're probably going to die at home because no one will be able to get to you."

I was going back and forth to Cedars for four to four and a half years starting from 2009. Dr. Elkin told me that from all the tests that he did he found there was something leaking inside my heart. He couldn't fix it. They think that during the second bypass that the graft was hit with a suture. Dr. Elkin was a cardiologist but not a surgeon. He wanted me evaluated by a number of doctors, not just him. Cedars hospital has teams of doctors and they operate in a group.

After the quad bypass, I had hiccups for two years and acid reflux. I had a defibrillator inside me as a safety measure while I had the dobutamine pump, which acts as caffeine for a dying heart, and waiting for the new heart. They cut my pectoral muscles and I lost my chest. I wore the pump for five years and it never went off. They were surprised because my ejection fraction was so low. I asked if I would still need the defibrillator after surgery and they assured me that I wouldn't. That's going- (they did remove it). You'll never need that again. When we put this new heart in you, you'll be a new person. The only thing is we won't be able to connect all the nerves. Some nerves just don't get connected again. You may feel a delay in your responses. You may process information a little differently. I'm kind of a slow motion guy anyway, so I haven't noticed this. I'm more laid back. I believe that if you go fast in life, you miss so much greatness.

Before the transplant, I had to lose one hundred pounds of muscle. I was skin and bones. It took about four months. I was mad and hungry! They used aggressive diuretics and a minimal nutritional diet. They were basically starving me. They brought me a bagel and two percent milk. It was like eating chalk off the sidewalk. It wasn't even a wheat bagel. Zero nutrition! I was so angry, I can't even tell you. I was starving.

"If you don't give me food, I'm out of here."

I got dressed. I took all my hospital stuff off.

"I'm starving, I don't feel well, and I'm out of here."

I put my pants on, my sweater, and my jacket. I got my luggage. The nurses were running after me. They chased me down the hallway.

"You can't just leave like that!"

"Watch me. I'm not in a wheelchair. I'm out."

They finally convinced me to stay.

They told me I was on NPO- no food or water.

They kept telling me that. They kept saying that they needed more blood, more tests.

"I don't have any blood left!" I was so angry I was beside myself.

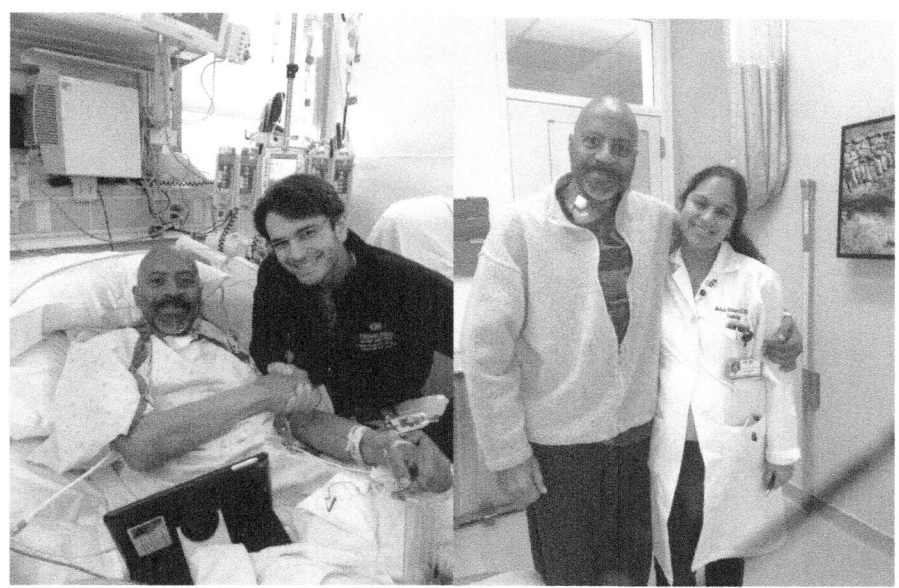

On November 22, 2014 I gave in and checked myself into the hospital at 6:00 in the evening. It was a busy emergency room. I had to wait, like four hours. They had mentioned to me to check in around this time of year because many people die around the holidays, which is an unfortunate truth. They said they did most of their transplants near Christmas.

At 2:00 AM on December 20, 2014, I got the phone call that would change my life forever. I could barely reach the phone.

I was literally skin and bones, 128 pounds. As I was reaching for it I fell out of bed and into the floor. I had it in my hand. It was the transplant office.

"Get excited, but not too excited! We found a heart that is tailor made for you. We need to do one more test when it arrives. We anticipate it will be fine and your team is coming to get you and prep you for surgery."

They had my photo on their wall as inspiration to help find my heart. They were all familiar with my case.

The doctors were having their Cedars Sinai Christmas party, when they located the heart for me. The transplant office was in conjunction with the doctors to review the heart. They all agreed that it was perfect for me. It was coming down from up north. They were going to get me in the room in four hours to prep me for transplant surgery.

Dr. Dannie Ramzy put my new heart in me.

He said, "You're in good hands."

I was scared as hell. I was so weak and out of it. I was horrified and didn't know what to expect next.

Dr. Ramzy is the protégé of Dr. Trintone, who was the original doctor who was scheduled to do the transplant. Dr. Ramzy was incredible and **saved my life.** A day or so later, I woke up to people saying, **"Oscar, we need you to wake up."**

Do you know your name? Do you know where you are? Do you recognize anyone? It's over. It's done. You have a new heart inside you right now."

"No really?"

I felt my chest and my defibrillator was gone.

"It's a new start. We have a lot of work to do. Your life will be changed forever."

"Can I ask? How old is the person whose heart I got?"

"Are you ready for this? You have the heart of a nineteen-year-old."

"How's that possible?"

I got excited, but I had tubes in my mouth. Everything faded to black again. I needed the breathing tube out. So the nurses ran and got the doctor and they pulled them out quickly. It was like God hit me on the back, like the Heimlich maneuver, to breathe on my own.

They were shocked that I was able to breathe on my own so early. The nightshift took care of this final near disaster.

When I went in for my check-ups, I would always see the nurse practitioner first. They would go over my meds and do blood pressure to get you ready for the doctor.

They were impressed with how few pills I was on.

I was on prednisone for about a year- just before and just after the transplant. But I weaned myself off of it slowly. I take two types of anti-rejection meds twice a day. I have to take this for the rest of my life.

When I was lying there in bed, worshipping every day, I would listen to this song, I Can Only Imagine. It goes like this: Surrounded by your glory, What will my heart feel, Will I dance for you Jesus, Or in awe of you be still, Will I stand in your presence, Or to my knees will I fall, Will I sing Halleluiah, Or be able to speak at all, I can only imagine, I can only imagine.

I am celebrating my new heart, which God gave me on Jesus's birthday, Christmas. I will make sure that I honor this heart. I can only pray that God gives me the opportunity to help others the way He has helped me.

Part of my plan is to start getting my music back again. My family wants to know about what happened to me and I'm going to get it to them in a big way. Johnny Taylor is my cousin. He used to sing with Sam Cooke.

Jesse Owens is my mom's first cousin. He was a four-time Olympic gold medalist in the 1936 Games. He was a track and field athlete.

I used to play for Shirley Caesar, the gospel singer, and Patti LaBelle. I did concerts with her when I was just a teenager.

I played bass. Edwin Hawkins Singers, the people who sang Oh Happy Day, I played with them, too, and so many others.

My Christmas gift from God, 2014

"We did not come to fear the future. We came here to shape it."

Barack Obama

Chapter 12
Big O Guest Speaker

An opportunity to talk to high school kids and share my story was given to me. I've been watching all the shootings on television: school shootings, police shootings, our innocent young people's lives shattered. I want them to be safe and do the right thing. I want them to make better decisions. I'll do whatever I can to help. If I can help set them on the right course, that's my job now.

A little advice:

This is what it is. I was you. I've been there. Instead of me taking my fists and whooping your little ass, I boxed Golden Gloves and have obtained black belts in two styles of Martial Arts.

A lot of the professional fighters came from the street. Many said "I need to do something with myself. I'm tired of being tired. No money in my pocket, a beat up old car… If you get tired of being tired, do something about it. Don't wait for someone else to help you."

I took up bodybuilding and it changed my life direction and thought process forever.

The dumbest thing I ever heard-"Where you from"? You all know that phrase. When you ask that question that means you have a problem yourself. You don't own the ground you're standing on when you ask that question. You don't own the neighborhood you live in. It ain't your block, but you and your boys call it your block. If someone comes in with a red shirt, or a black shirt or blue or whatever, you say let's kick his butt cause he has the wrong color on.

One day, that person is going to run up on the wrong person with the wrong shirt color, or neighborhood, and that person could be me. You will not be going home cause I'll break every bone in your body in ten seconds. I don't care how many of you there is. I don't need a gun either. If you pull a gun on me, I'll make you eat it. So, my point is, being tuff is really being tuff in your brain, because you did your homework. You have no fear. Whatever you're doing now in your life, you're creating the pathway for what you're going to become in the next two, three, four, five years. I come from a large family and not all of us are still alive.

God bless my brother, he didn't listen to me. He got caught up in a situation with his "friends", his homies. He chose to do that. I told him, "Brother, I love you. Choose some different friends. They're not good for you." As it turns out, he's unfortunately not here anymore and it huts everyday.

A little more advice: If you see the police approaching, do yourself a favor, pull the hoodie down. Let them see your face. Take your hands out of your pockets. When a cop rolls up on you and says stop, then stop cold. Leave your hands where they can see them. Don't move- don't scratch your head! Don't run, don't duck... this is how you stay alive. Roll your windows down so they can see who you are.

A lot of guys aren't going to do what I'm doing right now.

They say, "It ain't my problem, whatever."

But I'm not that guy. I'm the guy that says I want to help you, man.

Why do you have that look on your face?

Why are you angry? Or what's up with you?

Why are you all nervous? Talk to me. What's wrong?

Your posture says something to a police officer. A cop may see it as a threat. Each word that you use is indicative to what will happen to you in the next few minutes. If a cop pulls you over, it will probably only lasts a minute. They'll ask a question or two. The moment you say, "What you stopping me for? You put your hands on me, we're going to have a problem." At that point they may say, "Get on the ground. You're under arrest." Now you're going to jail, just because of what you said to the officer. Off duty or on duty, he has the power to lock you up if you are perceived as a threat to him.

Remember this, before you do anything, use this thing- **YOUR BRAIN**- that God gave you. This is your control tower, right here. Think, what's going to happen if I say what I'm thinking right now. How's this going to end? It's usually not in your favor. **There will always be consequences for your actions!**

If you have an attitude or a threatening manner, you are not going to win. Your brain keeps you alive. Your fists, elbows and all that are your backup. In reality, your posture dictates something about the person that you are. You may be walking down the street and someone may not like you because of your color or your race.

Check yourself before you leave the house every day. Remember those two words. Check yourself. Make sure you got no drugs in your pocket that you forgot from the night before, cause the moment you leave your house, a police officer has the right to check you, stop you, investigate, whatever.

If you think about stealing, robbing, think about 'what would happen to me if I get caught.' With all the cameras today, chances are you probably are going to get caught, cause there's cell phones everywhere, cameras on every building, every store, and every home. Somebody is seeing you, even with a hoodie on.

If you think that you can hide yourself with a hoodie, guess what? Your posture is not the same as the next guy.

You're walk, your shoe size, and your color pants you're easy to find in most cases. Don't think if you got away with it once that you would continue to get away with it.

Find something you love to do.

Train your mind in school and train your body outside of school.

You create your destiny based on the choices you make.

You control how your life is going to go. When you develop something inside yourself you have no more fear for the world. You are not a victim of circumstance.

When you strengthen your body, your mind gets stronger, too.

You become what you do and eat.

"Accept responsibility for your life. Know that it is you who will get you where you want to go, no one else."

Les Brown

Chapter 13
God Tracks

Each link in my life led to another and I didn't see any of it coming. I call it God tracks. Some people call it footprints in the sand. To me, when you're born and you're a special child, God allows different children, especially the quiet ones, an opportunity to become something great.

Life can be a journey and at the same time an obstacle course depending on your personal relationship with God. We all have gifts and talents; it's about finding and developing your relationship with Him.

Such as when a child opens up and starts to sing, people might say, "I didn't know you could sing."

"I never told anybody. I'd just sing in the bathroom."

"Why didn't you let me know?"

"I didn't know. I thought I was..."

"But you sound great!"

"You like it? Really?"

And they become great opera singers or whatever, not even realizing the talent that is within them. I was that kid. I knew I was good but I didn't know I was great.

My dad said, "Be great". I was living that life but I didn't think I was there yet. I'm not where I want to be yet. Even still.

When people say, "Dude, I've been watching you for thirty years. You guys in the Conan show are my idols."

I get that so much every day.

"If it weren't for you, I wouldn't be a football player. I wouldn't be playing for the NFL. You were instrumental. I used to come hang out with you guys at Universal Studios when I was a kid."

People who are busy don't even know how they're affecting people. We lay tracks and we almost forget how many tracks we lay behind us because we're too busy looking forward to where we want to be. That's how we got invited to this non-accidental meeting of the cast we had at Universal Studios. We were all meant to know each other and become lifetime friends. Fight like sisters and brothers on the stage with all our Conan secrets. What happens at the CASTLE stays at the CASTLE!

"Yeah, that's a nice car. You're doing all right. So you became a great man because I affected you, huh?"

You have no idea how many people you touch just by being you. I don't think that way because I'm busy looking forward. I'm not done. I'm not going to be done till I stop breathing.

Even at eighty, ninety, that's who you are going to be. All this is a conglomeration, divine destiny that God has given, this long-term journey that is life. And somewhere on this journey, some people go through extreme difficulties and don't understand why. It's all about making you great so God can fulfill his plan he has for you. He can't use you if you are not humble and available.

He needs great leaders to lead the ship because we change people whether we want to admit it or not. We are not patting ourselves on our backs, it's just true. It's a vibe that you transcend through strength, and creativity.

You see God hired me to work for him now. He's been trying to get my attention for years. I just refused to listen. He stopped me cold in my tracks. It's another trial he's putting you through but you refuse to listen.

Hello, it's God knocking on your door. You still don't get it yet? You can't do all your plans unless you listen to me.

So I began to pray relentlessly, 24/7. Gospel songs were on all day long. It takes the pain away. Our minds are amazing. All the pain in this world I was experiencing and it all went away with praise. I said I couldn't do this without you. If I wasn't listening before, you have my full attention now. I apologize.

You picked me to be a leader of men. Self will let you down. It will quit on you. If you don't pray about it, it may be all over. God snatched me from death, like a car hit me. I opened my eyes and I freaked out. I could only move my eyes. I looked around and was so happy to be back in the land of the living. I was born to be a

God Warrior. I knew this when I was a little boy. I just didn't know how to swing the sword yet.

(Philippians. 4:13) I can do all things through Christ who strengthens me.

I have these words on my phone. Am I pleasing you? If I'm going out, I want to make sure I'm connected to you. God has forewarned me. I see it.

Today I live in complete awareness, with God upfront!

Thank you for allowing me to share my story with you! I am grateful that God has given me another chance and I am committed to living a life, which honors him.

Oscar " Big O" Dillon

For more information please visit my website at

www.BIGODILLION.com

Made in the USA
Monee, IL
24 November 2021

82958844R00095